CONTENTS

ACKNOWLEDGEMENTS   vii

INTRODUCTION   ix

CHAPTER ONE: CONTESTED RATIONALE   1
1. Competing Purposes   2
2. Whose School? Which Catholicism?   9
3. Alternative Strategies and Priorities for Catholic   16
    Formation
4. Pluralism, Liberalism and Education   20
5. Criticisms of Holistic Worldviews   25
    Recommended Reading   29
    Notes   30

CHAPTER TWO: SCHOOL AS FAMILY   33
1. Family 'Capital'   34
2. Extended Families   40
3. Home–school Partnership   42
    Recommended Reading   49

CHAPTER THREE: SCHOOL AS BUSINESS   51
1. Strategic Planning and Customer Service   52
2. Resource Management   54
3. Market Forces   61
4. The Nature of Work   65
5. Managerialism in Education   73
    Recommended Reading   80

CHAPTER FOUR: SCHOOL AS CHURCH 81
1. Implications of Mission 82
2. Church Ethos before Vatican II 85
3. Theologies from Above and Below 87
4. Shift in Emphasis 90
5. Tasks and Obstacles 97
6. A School of the Gospel 109
   Recommended Reading 115
   Notes 116

CHAPTER FIVE: SCHOOL AS POLITICAL COMMUNITY 119
1. The 'Political' and Education 120
2. The Political Context and Role of School 123
3. School as a Political Community 129
4. Pluralism and Other Challenges 134
5. School as Institution and Community 137
6. In the Community and for the Common Good 140
7. The Political Dimension of School Leadership 146
8. Priorities for Catholic School Leaders 155
   Recommended Reading 159
   Notes 159

CHAPTER SIX: SCHOOL AS ACADEMY 163
1. The Centrality of Learning 165
2. Contested Curriculum 169
3. Contested Classrooms 182
4. Hospitable Spaces for Learning 185
5. Connections between Christian Teaching 196
   and Christian Learning
   Recommended Reading 207

CATHOLIC SCHOOLS
IN CONTENTION

Competing Metaphors and Leadership Implications

John Sullivan

VERITAS

First published 2000 by
Veritas Publications
7/8 Lower Abbey Street
Dublin 1

ISBN 1 85390 438 4

British Library Cataloguing
in Publication Data.
A catalogue record for
this book is available
from the British Library.

Cover design by Bill Bolger
Printed in the Republic of Ireland by Betaprint Ltd, Dublin

CHAPTER SEVEN: CONTRASTING POLARITIES   209
1. Objective and Subjective Approaches   210
2. From Rhetoric to Judgement in Education   218
    2.1. From Trust to Risk   218
    2.2. Pejorative or Positive Terms?   220
    2.3. Correlative Terms   221
    2.4. Rhetoric Reclaimed   222
    2.5. Judgement   225
3. Connections with Catholic Education   229
    Recommended Reading   232

CONCLUSION   235

APPENDIX   240

ACKNOWLEDGEMENTS

I am grateful to Dr Naylor, Principal of St Mary's College, Strawberry Hill, and to my line manager, Andy Phillips, for the flexibility and accommodation shown me with regard to the use of time across a busy working year. Without this degree of freedom and trust, the book could not have been written. Thanks are also due to my colleagues, Lesley King, a former primary-school headteacher, and Julie Clague, a moral theologian, to Geraldine Davies, Deputy Head of Bishop Thomas Grant Secondary School in Streatham, and Patrice Canavan, headteacher at Sion-Manning School in Kensington, all of whom read and commented helpfully on earlier drafts of different chapters.

Substantial parts of *Catholic Schools in Contention*, including some of the questions and tasks, have been read through and tried out by my MA students at both Brentwood and Twickenham, all of whom led me to hope that others too would find the book relevant to their practice. All of these students in our Catholic School Leadership course have been a delight to teach and I have learned much from them about the issues that continue to be 'live' for heads, deputies and senior staff in such schools. I hope that they will recognise – and take pleasure in – the degree to which many of the ideas articulated here reflect our discussions, arguments and reflections together.

Some of these ideas have also been tried out at international conferences, with helpful responses from representatives from Ireland, Scotland, the USA, Canada, Australia, South Africa, Scandinavia, Holland and Belgium. These responses confirmed my belief that the issues dealt with in this book and the complexities surrounding the move from the articulation of principles to their implementation, 'transfer' readily across many of the different national, regional and local contexts in which Catholic schools are set. This is despite the caveats and allowances one has to make for different constitutional, economic and cultural circumstances.

As usual in matters of writing, my wife and children have suffered from bouts of unavailability on my part, times when I have shouldered far less than my proper share of family responsibilities because of my desire to press on to completion. Apart from their tolerance, warmth and acceptance, which have helped me to proceed without the burdens of guilt or complaint, their contribution can be identified in those parts of chapter two that speak most positively about family life. I am very grateful to them for the loving space they have generously given me; I only hope that they feel that the outcome of my 'internal absences' is worthwhile. I was especially helped by my youngest child, Paul, who guided me, sometimes with great forebearing, in coping with some of the intricacies of the computer.

Finally, I am pleased to record my thanks to the staff at Veritas for all their encouragement, support and understanding as they have seen this book through from its initial proposal to publication.

INTRODUCTION

In this book I explore some of the leading ideas that appear to govern practice in Catholic schools, paying attention not only to their particular sources, shape and function, but also keeping in view their dynamic interaction. After a brief consideration of the currently contested rationale for Catholic schools, I examine some of the implications of viewing such schools in the light of the overarching metaphors of 'family', 'business', 'Church', 'political community' and 'academy'. At the heart of the work is an analysis of the implications, dilemmas and potential value clashes that emerge from the use of competing models and metaphors for school.

Far from being monolithic institutions, displaying identical features, like branch offices that receive instructions from central control or that work out of a blueprint intended to have universal application, Catholic schools exhibit diversity and pluralism and display a wide range of original syntheses in their responses to the ideas and values that compete for their allegiance. The richness offered by this diversity and originality derives in part from resources at the heart of the Catholic faith and in part from the sheer multiplicity in the cultural contexts, socio-economic circumstances and alternative ideologies that surround schools. Each chapter of this book brings to the fore some examples of the kind of responses that Catholic schools need to make to various overlapping communities to which they belong if they are to be true to their mission as well as to the realities of their situation.

A school is a very particular kind of place, institution and social gathering. Going to school for the first time is usually a landmark experience, both for parents and for their children.

The transition from primary to secondary school is often another crucial period of growth for students, frequently associated with a combination of feelings of anxiety, excitement and pride. Not only does going to school impel us into a new world, one with practices and priorities that differ from those we have already encountered, but also it is likely to transform our perspective on what has gone before. The school experience changes how we see the people we meet outside of school, how we interpret and respond to their words and actions. A reciprocal relationship exists between the habits and expectations developed in school and those that emerge from all the other social agencies and networks to which we belong. What we take from school and our capacity to benefit from it are both deeply influenced by our prior experiences and relationships, as well as by those that continue to be part of our lives. Such influences are usually a mixture of the benign and the less helpful. Similarly, and in parallel fashion, what happens in school makes a significant difference to how we perceive the hugely diverse and often competing invitations and pressures of the world around us, whether these be considered as opportunities to enjoy the 'goods' of life or as temptations towards the less worthwhile. In this respect, school can open many doors for us, both now and for later. It can either boost our confidence in ourselves and in the world, make possible countless opportunities for growth; or it can reinforce our prejudices, damage our self-esteem, cause us to have a fundamental distrust of others and imprison us in narrowness of outlook. Again, the effect of school on our involvement in other areas of life is usually a mixture of the positive and the negative.

As an important sphere of experience, school cannot operate in isolation from other spheres. Its purposes and possibilities, its functioning and effectiveness are all deeply penetrated, enhanced and constrained by alternative communities and agencies. Thus, a school is not a family. It has a different purpose from that of a family. It cannot offer many of the things that a family can. On the other hand, it should provide many things that a family usually cannot. In this book it is suggested that it would be a wise policy for school leaders to think carefully about the extent to which a school can and should reflect features of family life. Also, a school needs to take into account the real circumstances of the families it is working with, so as to build appropriately on this and to enable a healthy partnership between home and school to be developed. School 'as family' is the focus of chapter two.

Similarly, a school is not a business. It has a different mandate, relies on different methods, deploys different resources and aims for different outcomes. Nevertheless, without sufficient attention being paid to the 'business dimension' of educational institutions, schools would soon close and therefore fail in their own primary purposes. The world of work that surrounds a school will inevitably impinge upon its practices, offering both assistance and distractions. School leaders need discernment in distinguishing those features of the world of work that support their school's goals from those that undermine it. School 'as business' is the focus of chapter three.

Neither is a school the same as a church. To treat school and Church as identical in nature would be to distort either or both of them. The respective remit of each is different. For example, the kind of atmosphere that is legitimately to be expected in the classroom, attendance at which is compulsory for students, cannot be the same as might be looked for in a voluntary retreat house or in a local community's Sunday liturgy. Yet, in the context of Catholic schooling, there should be a close connection between Church and school. A Catholic school is part of the Church's mission; it will inevitably be influenced by current prevailing interpretations of what is meant by Church. A Catholic-school leader exercises a ministry within the Church and needs to maintain and develop a well-founded understanding of what this entails. School 'as Church' is the focus of chapter four.

Schools belong to and are usually authorised by national and local political communities. What is expected of schools and what it is possible for them to achieve can differ significantly according to the presuppositions that hold sway and the patterns of behaviour exemplified in these political communities. The political context will influence, for example, understandings of authority, styles of leadership, notions about rights, expectations about freedom and at least some of the virtues and skills desired as outcomes of schooling. Principals need to reflect on the relationship between their schools and the surrounding polity; if too negative, they jeopardise the future survival of the school; if too accommodating, they might be undermining its integrity and identity. Again, discernment is needed in distinguishing those features of political leadership that are relevant to school from those whose application would prevent its functioning as an educational community. School 'as political community' is the focus of chapter five.

Only in the light of an exploration of these earlier metaphors for school, as family, business, Church and political community, does it become possible to mark out more clearly the function of school 'as academy', as an ordered and hospitable space for learning. Policies and practices that rest on those metaphors of school analysed in chapters two to five can sometimes distract school leaders from educational considerations and deflect them from their primary goal, the promotion of learning. However, a lack of understanding about the sources and significance of such metaphors will almost certainly prevent appreciation of their limits as well as the extent of their applicability. In mapping out the principal ideological 'contours' of Catholic education this book is intended to help teachers to make sense of the conflicting demands upon them and to offer a resource that aids them in the task of acting wisely, both in the classroom and in school leadership. The promotion of learning, as the overriding priority for teachers and school leaders, is the focus of chapter six.

All educational communities must exemplify and facilitate a conversation about ideas and practices that are thought worthy objects of our attention and energy. There will always be creative tension in schools between, on the one hand, the 'content' to be communicated and those who speak 'for' it, the teachers, and, on the other hand, the readiness, capacity and desire of students to benefit from such 'content'. Effective teaching usually combines some form of 'structured novelty' – students are expected to know or to be able to do something different as a result of lessons – with human 'space-making' – sensitivity is shown to students' own perspectives, experience, feelings and sense of identity. Such effective teaching avoids a grinding and inexorable imposition of alien content as much as it avoids producing a warm, 'fuzzy' space that fosters merely an exchange of ignorance. In addressing the overlapping polarities of first, objectivity and subjectivity in education, and, second, the communicative qualities and skills of both teachers and students, chapter seven provides principles and guidelines for educational practice, which extend and complement those arising in earlier chapters.

I have drawn throughout this book on my own experiences. Family life, the 'business' of educational management, sharing in the mission of the Church, working as a senior officer in a highly politicised local government context, and teaching for many years – all these have contributed to one or more of the chapters here. My teaching experience began with young people; for the first twenty years of my career the average age of students in my classes was fourteen. During the last ten years my work has been with experienced and senior teachers; the average age of my students now is forty-eight! This more recent work is in the field of continuing professional development, in higher education and as an educational management consultant – mostly in the UK, but also with short stays in Ireland, the USA, Europe and Australia.

The audience I have kept most in mind throughout the writing has been these senior teachers, principals and assistant principals, who work as leaders in Catholic schools in the English-speaking world. It should also be relevant to several other target groups, such as those listed below:

- teachers in Catholic schools who aspire to positions of responsibility;
- diocesan officers who help in the selection of senior staff, and who monitor and inspect, advise and support those working in Catholic schools;
- board members/governors who represent the wider community and to whom principals are usually accountable;
- staff in higher education and in local authorities who offer in-service education and training for teachers;
- State and regional secular education policy-makers who work with Catholic schools as part of their brief;
- clergy and members of religious orders with an active involvement in Catholic education;
- parents who wish to understand the functioning, opportunities and constraints of Catholic schools (and perhaps to be more actively involved in partnership with them);

- Christians from other denominations who maintain their own schools or who have a close interest in the promotion of Christian education.

In addition to being heavily based on my practical experience, this book also draws freely from my eclectic (though, I hope, not undisciplined) reading and study in the fields of theology, philosophy of education, and the theory underpinning educational management. In this work I have been less concerned to test out the adequacy or internal consistency of any particular theory and more interested in exploring the potential (and limits) of key metaphors that not only illuminate the factors at work in schools, but that also have the motivating power and intellectual fertility to stimulate ideas and energy in the service of a better implementation of the mission of the Catholic school.

In order to clarify further the particular nature and the principal purpose of the book, let me make two comments, one about its contents and one about its possible use. First, nearly all the chapters combine three elements: in addition to my own reflections on the theme being explored, I provide a substantial and wide range of questions, plus a set of short extracts from other writers. These extracts illustrate or supply additional examples of themes under discussion.

Second, the work is intended to be interactive. I hope its readers will find that the organisation of the text prompts them to engage with the thoughts of the author, to relate these to their own experience, feelings and perspectives, to test the relevance and applicability of the suggestions made here to their own school, and to take into account ideas from other relevant writers whose work may be either unfamiliar or not easily available to school leaders. To this end, readers will probably derive most benefit if, instead of reading the book straight through, they stop at the appropriate places to answer for themselves the questions posed at regular intervals. These questions should assist readers in the process of engaging with the complex issues and creative tensions at the heart of the book, all of which relate to effective leadership in a Catholic school.

(ɔʋ) The work is also intended to facilitate interaction in another way, in the context of an extended postgraduate course in continuing professional development for Catholic school leaders, such as the various Master's programmes offered by many Catholic universities and colleges. Substantial personal and professional benefit can be gained by participating with a group of one's peers in a sustained period of further study. It can be very valuable to reflect on practice, its achievements and setbacks, its challenges and its disappointments, and to share with other committed believers the task of clarifying and promoting the mission of the Catholic school. When school leaders have a better understanding of the diverse pastoral situations that face Catholic schools, and when they deepen their appreciation of the ways in which others cope with the social, economic, technological, legal and political realities that influence educational institutions, they often find that they are able to identify new ways to tackle the gap that always exists between rhetoric and reality. Surrounded by a mutually supportive group ethos, it becomes easier for them to renew their commitment and to revitalise the inner sources of their motivation.

Catholic Schools in Contention is intended to accompany such a journey of reflection and sharing. The book will be more effective in achieving its aims if students, as they work through each chapter, take the time to write answers to the questions set as and when these arise, before continuing their reading. Further follow-up reading material is recommended at the end of each chapter. At least some of this reading should be completed in advance of the group's regular meeting, so that students are well-equipped to contribute to the conversation about principles and practice and their mutual bearing on one another. With their deliberations chaired and co-ordinated by a senior teacher, a diocesan officer or a university lecturer, the group could then share insights, compare answers, hear alternative experiences and perspectives, interrogate the text more deeply, raise further questions and assist one another in issues that arise from the further reading. Thus each chapter could form the basis of and serve as a study guide for a whole module within an advanced programme. I hope that this text, whether used for private reflection or as part of an extended course, will enable readers both to appreciate the significance of some of the controversies surrounding Catholic schools and to enter into these controversies with a renewed feeling of confidence.

CHAPTER ONE

CONTESTED RATIONALE

Catholic schools both echo and accentuate the ambiguities and conflictual nature of educational discourse carried on more generally. They share in and reflect closely some of the persistently heated and unresolved debates about educational values and priorities that pervade discussions about education, in other schools and in society as a whole. They also provide sites for additional and more complex value clashes. As arenas where competing personal and social expectations vie for attention and where multiple (and sometimes incompatible) religious and political 'models' (or interpretative frameworks) are operative, Catholic schools constitute an inherently interesting focus for a study of the bearing of ideology, principles and worldviews on education.

In this chapter, first I show that a Catholic school is a site in which many different purposes compete to achieve mastery. The Catholic school has no universally accepted single, overriding goal or priority. Second, I pick out some of the various principles, values, agencies and perspectives that jostle for attention, resources and control in Catholic schools. Third, some of the alternative strategies and priorities for Catholic formation are laid out. Fourth, in acknowledging that Catholic schools find themselves in a changed – and still rapidly changing – cultural context, some implications of Catholicism's encounter with pluralism are explored. In the final section I respond to important criticisms that have been levelled against faith-based forms of education.

1

1. COMPETING PURPOSES

All kinds of basic decisions in school life are inevitably affected by what are taken to be the main purposes of a school, the very reasons for its existence. Which students are to be admitted and which teachers are to be appointed, what kinds of learning are to be fostered and how resources are to be deployed, what kinds of behaviour are to be promoted and which types of activity are to be prohibited, how the school should be 'marketed' in the local community and how the work of staff and students is to be evaluated – answers to all these questions will be fundamentally dependent upon those purposes and goals that should underpin the life of the school.

Immediately questions arise: in whose eyes and according to whose perspective are these purposes to be derived? Will the purposes be those that are upheld by the State? What happens if there is a change of Government, and an accompanying change of priorities and policies? Should schools be ready to alter radically the direction they have taken in order to comply with new requirements? What if those in power do not adequately represent the wishes of the people? Can and, indeed, should schools stand out against unpopular measures, or are they agents for their paymasters?

Will the purposes be those of the parents who decide to send their children to one particular school rather than another? But, supposing their 'choice' is highly constrained by ignorance of alternatives, by inertia, by being subject to skilful manipulation or misleading information, or by factors relating to geographical location, ease of access, or financial costs, should their 'purposes' for the school be considered overriding, even if they have a common 'reason' to give for selecting the school?

Alternatively, should the purposes be identified and articulated by each particular school, leaving the public to decide first whether or not these aims represent congenial,

2

acceptable and worthy values to be pursued, and then whether or not they are being achieved in practice? A satisfactory answer to both these questions would presumably lead, other things being equal, to a choice of such a school for a son or daughter. But are decisions about the purpose (or purposes) of schooling to be left to the professionals alone? Do they have a monopoly of insight and wisdom in these matters? To what extent are they public servants, carrying out the wishes of the general public (in terms of the goals they pursue) by using particular and often specialised skills? Or is this to reduce teachers to technicians who carry out the instructions of others, without scope for initiative, discretion and judgement with regard to ends, using their intelligence only on the means selected to advance the projects assigned to them?

What degree of choice will be allowed to students themselves, at least for those in adolescence, as far as the goals, purposes, priorities and values of school are concerned? Will there be space for them to exercise their 'voice' in the direction of 'their' education? Or does this come only *after* formal schooling has finished, when they are sufficiently equipped in terms of knowledge, experience, maturity and so on?

It is clear that schools are places where purposes are contested. There is a constant struggle to contain and to re-focus the energies of students and continuing efforts are expended to elicit the allegiance of all members of a particular educational community to a set of values. Teachers, by dint of knowledge, experience, expertise and the authority invested in them, always represent a different world from that of their students. Part of their skill is shown in the various subtle ways they persuade the younger generation to engage seriously with the purposes and perspectives of the older generation, on whose behalf the school is founded. In one way or another teachers hope to make learning accessible, attractive, meaningful and transforming, in the process overcoming reluctance, resistance, fear, lack of confidence, distrust and difficulty.

Inevitably, teachers are 'political' creatures. They must secure the 'vote' of attention; they must mobilise the energies of young people in service of a particular cause; they must exercise influence deliberately. If they are to be effective in this, they must anticipate opposition before it surfaces and take steps to minimise its impact, if they cannot outmanoeuvre or deflect it entirely. This kind of contest has always been a feature of schooling, even when a significant congruence between the purposes of the adults within and beyond the school could be obtained. It is a task (and a contest) that is much more complex and demanding now that so many different purposes and priorities for schools are jostling for acceptance and where the value-laden nature of education operates so frequently out of controversy rather than consensus.

I am not merely suggesting that education provides a context where these various parties compete in order to get their way, as if they were made up of homogeneous blocks. On the contrary, there are huge differences among politicians, parents, teachers and students. Furthermore, the stances and concerns of each are constantly being modified in the face of overlapping and mutually interacting contexts, at the personal, local, national and international levels, including the family, society, the economy, technological developments, political groupings, the cultural climate, mass media and the philosophies and lifestyles that are plausibly available at any particular time.

There continues to be widespread disagreement about the relative priority to be attributed to different purposes for schools. Are they to serve democracy, by equipping students to become informed and responsible citizens? Are they to serve the economy, by equipping students to contribute efficiently to the workforce? Are they places for the promotion of knowledge, passing on the foundations of the various disciplines and equipping people to continue to be lifelong learners? Are they places that foster self-knowledge, the ability to identify for oneself a direction for life and a capacity to pursue this intelligently, the desire to find one's own sources of motivation and meaning and to grow in the art of self-expression? Are they places intended to make possible harmonious community life amidst a plurality of cultures, races and belief-systems?

Whichever one of these receives emphasis in a particular school, there are certain practical implications that follow. These include the kinds of teachers appointed, the way the school is run (both in terms of responsibility structure and of 'tone'), the allocation of time, the distribution of resources, the forms of measurement (and reporting) of student progress that are adopted, together with the nature of institutional accountability expected.

1. Of the following, who should be involved in the decision to appoint a teacher to a particular school: parents, students, politicians, other teachers, the head/principal of the school, other representatives of the local community, and/or from Higher Education, others? (Justify who you include and who you leave out.)

2. In your view, what are the three most important requirements/qualities of a teacher for the kind of school you would want for your own children?

3. Which purposes for your ideal school could not be met by an alternative educational strategy of providing state-of-the-art computer facilities in every home?

4. If you were put in charge of a new school, with a healthy budget, what three items would receive high priority from you, thereby showing your priorities? Explain your decision.

5. If you had to make a judgement as to whether to send your child to a particular school, what evidence would be relevant?

Education is best conceived of as a thermostatic activity. ...Education tries to conserve tradition when the rest of the environment is innovative. Or it is innovative when the rest of the society is tradition-bound. ...The function of education is always to offer the counter-argument, the other side of the picture. ...The school stands as the only mass medium capable of putting forward the case for what is not happening in the culture. ...Where, for example, a culture is stressing autonomy and aggressive individuality, education should stress co-operation and social cohesion. Where a culture is stressing conformity, education should stress individuality. (Neil Postman, *Teaching as a Conserving Activity* [New York: Dell, 1979], pp. 25, 27.)

6. What do you think of this view of education? In which areas of life is our society 'overdosing' and requiring some balancing act by schools?

[Thomas Jefferson] believed that the goal of schooling should be to help people protect themselves against \tyranny. ...[Marshall McLuhan] said: education will become recognized as civil defense against media fallout. (Postman, 1979, pp. 102, 82.)

7. To what extent are these purposes for school (a) necessary, (b) possible, (c) intimately related?

The goal agenda of the schools is so full, so complicated, even so contradictory that almost nothing of enduring value can be accomplished. ...If you heap upon the school all of the problems that the family, the church, the political system, and the economy cannot solve, the school becomes a kind of well-financed garbage dump, from which very little can be expected except the unsweet odour of failure. ...Schools should not, except under the most extreme provocation, try to accomplish goals which other social institutions traditionally serve. ...Teachers are not competent to serve as priests, psychologists, therapists, political reformers, social workers, sex advisers, or parents. (Postman, 1979, pp. 103, 107.)

8. Is it possible explicitly to reject some of the priorities or purposes being pressed on schools, and, if so, which ones would you be seeking to 'keep at bay'?

George Bernard Shaw asserted: art should refine our sense of character and conduct, of justice and sympathy, greatly heightening our self-knowledge, self-control, precision of action and considerateness, and making us intolerant of baseness, cruelty, injustice, and intellectual superficiality and vulgarity. (Quoted by Postman, 1979, p. 139.)

9. How happy would you be with this as a description of the function of education in your school? Which parts of this description seem most closely to match the reality of current achievement in your school?

In a fundamental sense, all arguments about how education ought to be conducted are arguments about the validity of competing metaphors [metaphors about human nature, the human mind, the role of school, the nature of teaching and learning, etc.]. ...Some think of school as a prison; others, a hospital; still others, a military organization, or an extension of the home. ...Are students patients to be cared for? Troops to be disciplined? Sons and daughters to be nurtured? Inmates to be punished? Resources to be cultivated? Personnel to be trained? (Postman, 1979, p. 143).

10. What are the leading metaphors relating to school that are actually operating 'behind the scenes' among your students, teachers, administrators, parents and governors/Board of Management?

Education is more a matter of search than one of conformity. [It should encourage us to] submit to a searching questioning those beliefs and outlooks – about justice, morality, religion, politics, etc. – which have become the prevailing order of a particular *polis*, or community. ...The unattainability of certainty is a basic feature of the human condition, ...a wholehearted acknowledgement of this is among the most important of educational virtues. (Padraig Hogan, *The Custody and Courtship of Experience* [Dublin: The Columba Press, 1995], pp. 29, 134).

11. How do you see the relative position of (or the balance to be established between) conviction, commitment and questioning in the years of schooling?

The idea of public education depends absolutely on the existence of shared narratives *and* the exclusion of narratives that lead to alienation and divisiveness. ...[By a narrative I mean] not any kind of story, but one that tells of origins and envisions a future, a story that constructs ideals, prescribes rules of conduct, provides a source of authority, and, above all, gives a sense of continuity and purpose. [This story] has sufficient credibility, complexity, and symbolic power to enable one to organize one's life around it. ...Without narrative, life has no meaning. Without meaning, learning has no purpose. Without a purpose, schools are houses of detention, not attention. (Neil Postman, *The End of Education* [New York: Vintage, 1996], pp. 17, 5, 7.)

2. WHOSE SCHOOL? WHICH CATHOLICISM?

In Catholic education there are additional dimensions to the contest over the rationale for schools. These additional dimensions include questions of authority and control, different perspectives on the relative weight to be given to different aspects of Catholicism itself and disagreement about the central role of a Catholic school.

With regard to the first of these, there are, potentially, tussles between the respective jurisdiction of Canon and Civil Law. Different priorities can be uppermost in the minds of the local bishop, the parish priest (often a governor or member of the Board of Managers) and diocesan education officers. Local or national education inspectors and officers, teachers and their unions, perhaps even parents, may not always agree with diocesan policy (for example, about the criteria for senior teacher positions, or about the merits of self-government for a school).' In some cases, religious orders, who can own the land and property, act as trustees, provide or appoint the staff, or offer an inspirational ideology and charism that underpins the whole educational enterprise in a particular school, may take a different view from that held by other partners in education.

This position is further complicated when one takes account of the fact that some religious orders have their headquarters in countries other than that in which the school is located and could operate from principles and priorities that differ in either minor or even significant ways from custom and practice in 'their' schools. Nor can it be assumed that episcopal educational policy will be identical in each diocese. There have been cases when actions taken in one diocese to protect or advance the cause of Catholicism in schools have been considered unacceptable in another, for example, with regard to appropriate textbooks or programmes of study, or with regard to the enforcement, if necessary through dismissal, of teachers who do not comply with expected standards of behaviour or lifestyle.

These disputes are not just about who has the final say when conflict emerges. They are intimately connected to serious disagreement about priorities and emphases within Catholicism itself. For example, cases where particular teaching resources have been rejected as unsuitable for Catholic schools, or where particular teachers have been dismissed (on religious rather than professional grounds) are often the focus of fierce disputes among the Catholic community. What some take to be a major cause of scandal and an impossible obstacle to the promotion of Catholic education, others accept as part of the pattern of human weakness and as open to forgiveness and acceptance for the sake of the greater good. A person with shortcomings in one aspect of life may still be able to offer important positive witness in many other ways. To include in one's community a sinner no more defends or advocates as worthy that person's sins than it would in the wider context of Church life.

Part of the contest here is the respective weight to be given to a prophetic, as opposed to a pastoral approach to people and issues. The prophetic approach upholds the truth and condemns error; it carries out these tasks with courage, clarity and consistency. It advocates what is right and good without being hampered by considerations of popularity or how difficult it might be to live up to the ideals espoused. It is ready to condemn whatever and whoever falls short in order to save perpetrators (from themselves) as well as victims. In confident possession of the truth, it is ready to pass judgement, prefers cut-and-dried solutions, is distrustful of compromise and is unready to turn a blind eye to shortcomings. Behind this prophetic stance is an understanding of the transcendent nature of God, a God who supremely escapes all our categories and who is always beyond us, a God who calls us to perfection, who challenges us to grow in holiness. The prophetic stance has great virtues but it can slip into harshness and exclusivity.

On the other hand, Christians also believe that God is immanent, intimately close, constantly forgiving and, in a mysterious way, ready to wait upon and be vulnerable to our slowness to respond. From this picture of God, a more pastoral approach seems called for, one that is ready to forgive

11

shortcomings, is slow to judge or condemn, and that accepts people where they are at a particular time.

Both approaches find warrant in Scripture. If a limb causes you to sin, cut it off. I have come to bring fire and the sword. Yet also, don't root up the weed before the harvest. Put up your sword. The Church constantly faces the paradox that steps taken to defend or to advance the truth can so easily undermine the good and portray its advocates in a most unattractive and unworthy light. Coercion, whether through social and moral pressure to conform or to leave, or through the support of law, leaves an unsavoury taste, rarely builds up the community and often casts a shadow over the good that is at stake. Both its victims and its victors are in some way damaged and diminished in the process. Authoritarian enforcement of conformity seems a strange way to demonstrate faith and forgiveness. This strangeness is further underlined when pressure seems to be applied mainly in areas of sexual misconduct or doctrinal unorthodoxy, as if these were to be considered as of overriding importance in Christianity.

From the richness of Catholicism, where should attention be focused first, given that it is the task of a lifetime to appreciate the fullness of the faith? Should we concentrate mainly on doctrine, its shape and structure, its key elements and core concepts? Even in this, should we attend more to doctrines held in common with other Christians or to those that seem distinctive to Catholicism? How seriously can and should the ecumenical imperative be taken in the school context? Or should the priority be given to developing appropriate habits for prayer and vibrant and regular experiences of worship? Even here, what is an appropriate blend of traditional and experimental? Is the priority to start with the creation of a Christian community, so that students experience for themselves the ethos, tone, climate, atmosphere, rules, habits, celebrations, give and take, the burdens and benefits, the responsibilities and opportunities offered by belonging to a particular community inspired by the gospel? How outward-looking should such a community be, if it is truly to display a Christian mentality? If it is too inward-looking, concerned with its own health and soundness, this can slip into exclusivity, narrowness, preciousness, isolation, thereby encouraging selfishness rather than service.

The contested rationale for the Catholic school can be described in other ways. We might consider *who it is for* and also what is envisaged as its principal debating partners and threats. Are Catholic schools primarily to support Catholic parents in their task of bringing up their children in the faith? Are they intended to be places that nurture faith, witness to it, teach about it, where the teachers embody, proclaim and facilitate the more abundant life in Christ for the sons and daughters of those who wish this? If this is the case, what constitutes a critical mass of Catholic students and staff, to allow this nurturing role, this conveying of the faith, to have a reasonable chance of happening? (It can never, of course, be guaranteed.) Or, are numbers irrelevant: does it affect the nature of a Catholic school if a significant percentage of its members do not share the Catholic faith? In such cases, does it become more important that the staff can offer powerful witness, consistency and clarity of Catholic teaching and practice?

On the other hand, there are Catholic schools where the main emphasis has simply to be on addressing the needs, educational and spiritual, of the local community. According to this approach, service is the primary feature of Catholic schools, which function as examples of the Church's concern to contribute to the upbuilding of the world as well as of the Kingdom. To concentrate on a broader notion of service, rather than on nurturing Catholicism explicitly, is not a contradiction of that first possible aim; but it does constitute a different approach. For example, criteria for student admissions may well need to be modified (with Catholicity having a lower profile) and the content of the curriculum may have a different configuration (with greater attention to meeting the spiritual needs of students who are not Catholics). Adopting service as a major priority could well lead to a situation where some assumptions influencing Catholic education will be challenged. To a certain extent, without undermining any of the key elements in Catholicism, the Second Vatican Council called upon the Church to address the hopes and fears and to serve the deepest needs of their fellow humans, to risk going out into the world as pilgrims and to co-operate with others as much as possible, rather than retreating into a safe fortress, however sacred it may be.

A third possible way of envisaging Catholic schools, especially in societies that are rapidly becoming simultaneously both more deliberately secular and more consciously multicultural, is as places for prophetic, counter-cultural witness. Seen in this light, Catholic schools will challenge those prevailing values and priorities of society that compete for our allegiance, for example, success and self-expression, materialism and hedonism, individualism and managerialism, sexism and racism. A Catholic education will witness to alternative values and demonstrate the possibility of a different lifestyle from those being adopted in the wider society. It will prick complacency where the Church has become too closely entwined in the social or political structure; it will equip its 'graduates' to tackle forthrightly injustice wherever it is encountered, to swim against the tide, to resist pressure to conform, to be discerning about the messages conveyed to them, for example, through the various communications media.

The student in such a school would require a curriculum, a training and a community experience that explicitly took these expected outcomes into account.

To adopt any one of these three major versions of Catholic schools, as nurturing faith, as offering service, or as counter-cultural forces, does not rule out the others, but it does give a different slant on and emphasis to the kind of education being sought. There is a creative tension between these different approaches. They imply different allies, different enemies, different resources and different priorities.

12. Using a traditional metaphor, let (a) the field represent the students and their personal and social circumstances, let (b) the seed represent the message(s) we have to bring, (c) the sowers stand for the teachers and their personal and social circumstances, (d) the sowing implies all the processes and practices involved in education, and (e) the harvest stands for the outcomes, especially long-term, that we hope will result from our work in schools. In which of these five, in your experience, has there been the most change in Catholic schools?

13. A motto is an extremely compressed form of message that frames the purpose or ethos of an organisation or school. Which of the following possible mottos for a Catholic school do you find least attractive and which most attractive and why?

- **Victory over sin**
- **Walk in the Light**
- **Witnesses for Christ**
- **Preparing for death**
- **Turning the world upside-down**
- **Servants of the Word**

14. What three personal qualities/capacities do you consider essential 'ingredients' in a good Catholic man or woman?

15. In your view, which of the following factors most contributes to the special character of a church school and why: (a) size/numbers; (b) local environment; (c) student intake; (d) composition of staff; (e) whoever owns and/or controls the school; (f) accommodation and resources; (g) external pressure and support?

16. Which factor, internal or external to the school, in your view most makes Catholic education difficult to sustain or to flourish?

3. ALTERNATIVE STRATEGIES AND PRIORITIES FOR CATHOLIC FORMATION

The continued existence of and rationale for Catholic schools should never be taken for granted by those who exercise leadership in them, even where society seems to accept or, more positively, to welcome them. The Church has not always advocated the necessity of a specifically Catholic school system. There may come a time when this is not seen as necessarily the right way forward, or at least not as the *only* possible strategy for upbringing and formation in the faith. Sermons, liturgy, catechesis, sodalities, sacramental participation, religious literature, pilgrimages, Scripture study and other forms of adult and higher education are also available for individuals' and group's religious and spiritual development. Catholic schools may essentially be good, but they should never be seen as something ultimate or of supreme and unquestioned value. This would be to lose sight of their provisional, at best penultimate, position, in service of a larger purpose, which may, in some contexts and at different times, allow for, even demand, alternative approaches to Christian formation and to the Church's influence on education.

Some already question the wisdom of relying on a separate Catholic school system as the principal type of Church involvement in education, either on the grounds that this strategy completely fails to reflect the ecumenical imperative, as outlined, for example, by Pope John Paul II in *Ut Unum Sint* (1995), or simply on the grounds that the Catholic school system cannot 'deliver', or cannot *any longer*, because of changed circumstances, meet the hopes that have been invested in it. According to this view, Catholic schools are rather like bouncing cheques, which cannot be relied upon to yield hard currency in terms of expected outcomes when they are drawn on. Their account is 'empty', and our energies should be redeployed elsewhere, if we are prudently to read the signs of the times. A new pastoral strategy for education, for example, parish renewal, small group-work, base communities, family networks, study circles, self-governing action-focused cells, might offer more scope and greater flexibility in responding to current needs, constraints and opportunities.

School leaders should also be alert to the objections to separate Catholic schooling that could possibly be raised by secular critics on economic, social, political and educational grounds. Insofar as it is compatible with Catholic education, such leaders should endeavour to demonstrate that their schools (a) offer value for money, making efficient and effective use of public resources; (b) do not reinforce existing divisions within society, but instead enhance mutual understanding between different social groups; (c) promote responsible citizenship and positive involvement in the life of the nation; and (d) foster critical and independent thinking across a broadly based curriculum.

Leaders who are aware of the essentially contested purposes of their schools, who listen carefully to criticisms, objections and calls for alternative strategies, so long as they are not paralysed through their encounter with these views, are less likely to ride roughshod over doubters and dissidents among staff and students. They are also less likely to appear complacent about the merits of their school. At the same time they should be more likely to be sensitive to gaps between rhetoric and reality, seeking to reduce these wherever possible. One might hope, too, that their awareness of the precarious nature of a deep and sustained consensus about and commitment to the mission and espoused aims and values of the school will prompt them to work constantly to breathe life into these, so that they truly attract and guide staff and students and inspire them to engage such aims with enthusiasm.

> [Catholic education requires that] all the teachers unite their educational efforts in the pursuit of a common goal. Sporadic, partial, or uncoordinated efforts, or a situation in which there is a conflict of opinion among the teachers, will interfere with rather than assist in the students' personal development. (Congregation for Catholic Education, *The Religious Dimension of Education in a Catholic School* [London: Catholic Truth Society, 1988], 99.)

17. How contested is the rationale for Catholic education in your school?

> The Catholic school must be open to the modern world and modern culture – no longer being inward-looking or exclusivist. Consequently the Catholic school must be in critical dialogue with modern culture, affirming what is

> positive about modernity... while at the same time negating the destructive dimensions of modernity. The Catholic school of the future ought to be distinctive in its critical openness to the... world, prominent in promoting ecumenical activity, and active in the embrace of inter-Faith dialogue. (Dermot Lane, *The Future of Religion in Irish Education* [Dublin: Veritas, 1997], pp. 131-7.)

18. (a) How do you see a balance being maintained by your school between, on the one hand, nurturing a sense of strong identity within it and, on the other hand, encouraging openness and outreach from it? (b) Which developments in society do you want your school to affirm and which to oppose? (c) How do you envisage your school contributing to ecumenism and inter-faith dialogue?

> Catholicism has shown itself capable of making people feel like hopeless sinners instead of affirming their essential goodness; of controlling their experience of God's presence instead of nurturing their sacramental consciousness; of encouraging sectarianism, racism, and patriarchy instead of communities of openness, equality, and mutuality; of repeating as closed a culture-bound tradition instead of drawing new life from it; of practising authoritarianism and blind obedience instead of a chosen faith and informed conscience; of practising shallow pieties instead of deep spiritualities; of working hand-in-glove with oppressive regimes and acquiescing in privileged social status instead of working for justice and social transformation; of encouraging parochialism instead of catholicity, narrow mindedness, exclusion, and

> prejudice instead of openness and hospitality. ...Catholic
> schools must confront their lack of catholicity. (Thomas
> Groome, *Educating For Life* [Allen, Texas: Thomas More,
> 1998], pp. 43-4, 413.)

19. What is your response to this challenging comment? Which potential criticisms are *least* true of your school? Is it possible to identify one area where your school could become more Catholic/catholic?

4. PLURALISM, LIBERALISM AND EDUCATION

One factor that has influenced Catholics' understanding of their faith in relation to others – and therefore also how they conceive the task of Catholic education – is their encounter with pluralism, especially in the context of liberal democratic societies. In the early 1960s, when Catholics were increasingly seeking closer involvement in and acceptance from the societies in which they were situated, a new rationale was sought that might justify a more positive accommodation to non-Catholic cultures. The American theologian John Courtney Murray was quick to learn from his fellow Jesuit, the Canadian Bernard Lonergan, about the significance of a shift from a classicist understanding of culture to one that was both more historically conscious and sensitive to pluralism.

Lonergan described classicist education as a matter of 'models to be imitated, of ideal characters to be emulated, of eternal verities and universally valid laws'.[1] Such an approach treats circumstances as accidental and it values stability, fixity and immutability. It does not allow proper scope for living tradition or for inclusiveness. It adopts an oppositional stance towards the world and fails to take proper account of the reality of pluralism. Lonergan identifies three sources of pluralism: it stems from linguistic, social and cultural differences, from the degree to which differentiation of consciousness with regard to the various realms of thought and endeavour has been achieved, and from the presence or absence of intellectual, moral or religious conversion.[2] It is clear from all the essays written during the final fifteen years of his life (he died in 1984) that Lonergan was urging his Church to recognise and respond adequately to the presence of pluralism and to apply such a response in any attempt to enter into dialogue about religious matters or to communicate the faith.[3] Lonergan treated pluralism as a positive feature of our world, not one that must be regretted or resisted.[4]

The philosopher John Kekes also sees pluralism in a positive light: 'the plurality of values enriches the possibilities for our living good lives, increases our freedom, motivates us to assert greater control over the direction of our lives, and enlarges the repertoire of conceptions of life that we may recognise as good'.[5] However, pluralists appear to present two difficulties to a Catholic perspective. Built into a pluralist outlook there reside two related assumptions that are questionable: first, a denial that there can be any authoritative system of values or any particular value that should be treated as overriding; and second, the notion that an individual life can be represented as a work of art, to be devoted and crafted solely according to the wishes of the 'artist'.[6] The first assumption clashes with the moral claims of the Church to be the divinely authorised interpreter and guardian of revelation and to be a community of moral wisdom. The second assumption relies too much on a sense of self-sufficiency and thereby fails to do justice to the effects of sin in our lives and our need for grace and the guidance of the Church. It also seems to imply a subjectivist position in ethics.

Kekes reminds us that within the prevailing liberalism of our society there are several contenders or foci for key values, these being rights, justice, equality and freedom.[7] These values will sometimes conflict and it will not always be clear how to resolve such conflicts. Such pluralism makes it difficult to separate out smoothly, as liberals often wish to do, those values that can be called substantive and those that are procedural, those that are of intrinsic value and those whose value is merely instrumental.[8] The attempt to keep to a minimum the number of procedural, instrumental, perhaps better expressed as 'space-making' values, in order to facilitate the broadest and most easily arrived at consensus, may lead to an artificial division between different types of values and the purchase these have in people's lives and the role they play within the diverse characters of individuals and communities. The 'thin', procedural values of liberals actually trade off the moral capital or residue of much more substantive personal and communal values, for example, self-discipline, self-sacrifice, law abidingness, order, stability and continuity, a sense of belonging, social responsibility and solidarity.[9] To the extent that this is so, the maintenance of more substantive or 'constitutive' communities may be an important, perhaps even necessary means of preserving sufficient 'back-up' or motivational and moral support for the continued healthy operation of space-making virtues such as tolerance and respect.

20. What impact, if any, has the encounter with pluralism had on your own school or in your own professional experience? Have you felt this impact more as a threat or as an opportunity?

The space-making effect of an acceptance of pluralism need imply neither relativism nor subjectivism, both of which are incompatible with the objectivist view of morality held within

Catholicism, but it does prevent a dogmatic absolutism, whether by Church or by the State. To this extent, one can argue that, if the claim by Catholics to a distinctive philosophy of education is not to entail more than the minimum level of exclusiveness required to maintain identity, then an acceptance of pluralism will be a necessary feature of any attempt to combine such distinctiveness with inclusiveness.[10]

The acceptance and application of pluralism within the Catholic community, with regard to its own members, who display a pluralism of stances towards the Church's teaching and a diverse range of stages in their own moral and religious development, will in some ways prove more difficult than the Church's acceptance of pluralism in the wider society. In the case of the latter, the Church has no social or political mandate to impose its views on others, nor a duty to establish orthodoxy or orthopraxy (other than its general mission to spread the gospel) and must exercise restraint instead of interfering in the lives of others, first as a mark of respect for individual dignity and freedom and, second, because it wants this forbearance to be reciprocated by outsiders in regard to the Church's conduct of her own affairs. Yet, inevitably, there will be tension between the rights of individuals to self-expression within the community of faith and the rights of that community to maintain rules for the preservation of its identity, priorities and purpose. This tension overlaps but does not coincide with a parallel tension between the 'universalising' and the 'particularising' functions of education.[11] I take this to mean that education must equip students with the necessary knowledge, concepts, skills, attitudes and habits so that they are enabled to belong to, to benefit from and to contribute to the wider society of which they are members, and also that it must enable them to participate in the smaller, more localised, perhaps minority subcultures and communities from which they derive their identity. Increasingly, this will demand a form of social and moral 'bilingualism'. Such 'bilingualism' should be enriched and strengthened if students experience in their education a healthy balance of emphases between fostering a confident individual perspective and a sense of the importance of co-operation and teamwork.

The acceptance of pluralism and its ascription of rights to groups and minority cultures (of which Catholicism is an example) leave open the possibility that the rights of parents or of the Church might oppressively outweigh the individual rights of young people for a reasonable amount of psychological 'space' in which to explore the 'boundaries' of their beliefs, to experiment, or to criticise their own tradition. Amy Gutmann observes that 'group recognition ties individuals too tightly to scripts over which they have too little authorial control' and she asks 'can there be a politics of recognition that respects a multitude of multicultural identities and does not script too tightly any one life?'[12]

I think that the claim to offer a distinctive and substantive philosophy of education is quite compatible with an acceptance of Gutmann's warning against 'scripting' that is too tight, since this would undermine students' dignity and render them passive and ultimately not responsible for their decisions and actions. At the same time, however, there would have to be limits on how loose the 'script' could afford to be, without dissolving into a series of disconnected soliloquies, the particular 'play' or 'plot' from which the scripts emerge as adaptations, for 'to be autonomous is not to be free-floating, but to be always engaged or potentially engaged in a kind of dialectic between reflectiveness and embeddedness. The inculcation of settled standards in early life is as much a prerequisite for this as the nurture of the critical faculties'.[13]

5. Criticisms of Holistic Worldviews

Various criticisms have been levelled against the attempt to offer a comprehensive, substantive or holistic worldview and morality. Some of these criticisms are justified, but others should be refuted. In each case Catholics would be wise to consider the degree to which these criticisms have a bearing upon their own claim to offer a distinctive philosophy of education.

Four examples are given by Bhikhu Parekh, who calls such an approach 'monist'.[14] First, moral monism assumes that the final truth has been discovered. Second, it teaches that one way of life is the best. Third, it is inhospitable to differences and breeds a spirit of intolerance. Fourth, it misunderstands other ways of life by adopting a judgemental approach to them, and at the same time distorts its interpretation by concentrating on how they are similar to or different from its own position.[15]

With regard to the first criticism, it might be argued that, while Catholics, along with their fellow Christians, do believe that a definitive, essential and salvific message of truth has been revealed by God, built into this belief is faith in the continuing presence of the Holy Spirit, part of whose work is to lead us into truth ever more fully. This entails the view that there is more truth to be discovered. (Though we should not forget that the constant, Spirit-led, revealing of truth and our deeper penetration into it and appropriation of it, does not render it less mysterious.)

With regard to the second criticism, it is clear that if we do overprivilege one way of life, we might be tempted to ignore the huge variety or pluralism within the combination of skills, values and virtues needed for good lives in the diverse circumstances we experience. Parekh brings out that life, especially life that is truly social, depends on a flexibility as well as a combination of values, and that such a flexibility and combination is facilitated if we enjoy access to other cultures.

'Cultural diversity encourages humility, modesty, self-knowledge, objectivity and self-transcendence.'[16] Catholics must then guard against any tendency within their tradition towards complacency and any temptation to be inward-looking, both of which would display exclusiveness in the form of unwarranted pride, rigidity and unwillingness to learn from others. Whatever community we belong to, it is wise to question the unity of 'us' and the otherness of those we label 'other'.[17]

The third and fourth criticisms, about intolerance and distortion, are intimately connected to the narrowness and blindness and other defects that are part of a claim to have established a definitive way of life for all to follow. If we are open to cultural differences, we are less likely to display the narrowness of the monist approach and more likely to create the conditions in which both communities and individuals can reconstitute themselves through creative responses to what is 'outside' of them.

In a pluralist society there will inevitably be tensions created through the interplay between pressures for cultural loyalty, the exigencies of critical reflection and the requirements of citizenship. My brief consideration of Parekh's criticisms of monism has shown that cultural loyalty and the Catholic community's self-understanding will be both challenged and enriched by having to demonstrate openness to 'otherness'. The challenge and enrichment, however, are reciprocal, for many of the qualities that are built up by and required for a committed cultural loyalty are also needed for citizenship in a plural society. This is sometimes insufficiently appreciated when holistic views are criticised for leading to a deficient view of education and an inadequate preparation for democratic citizenship.

In response to Halstead's attempt to allow more room for cultural attachment than is usually granted within liberal education, Burtonwood makes several criticisms that appear unjustified.[18] It is not necessarily true that the desire to preserve a culture or tradition leads to the denial of individual agency, to understating internal differences, or to neglecting change, although these are all possible dangers.[19] In the case of the Catholic Church, the whole experience of the Second Vatican Council and its aftermath shows that greater respect for the dignity of individual freedom, greater recognition of the pluralism of cultures within the Church and a more positive attitude towards change can all be accommodated by a faith community with a strong desire to preserve authoritative tradition, Scripture, beliefs and teachings. Although those who adhere to substantive and comprehensive moralities and belief-systems *may* be tempted to conflate personal and cultural identity, this can also be a temptation to which they do not yield, even if it is conceded that their sensitivity about this matter is one they have learnt from secular or liberal critics.

Nor is it the case that parts of a culture cannot be criticised without bringing into question the whole.[20] It *may* be the case that *some* criticisms of a belief system are so damaging that the whole edifice collapses as a result, but frequently a tradition, a culture or a belief-system can accommodate criticism with integrity and without contradiction, in a way that allows both continuity and innovation.

One can accept Burtonwood's point that the capacity to transcend cultural frameworks, which would surely be a feature of the critical reflection fostered by liberal education, will loosen our attachment to them, in the sense that we would be distanced from them in the very act of criticism and comparison with other points of view.[21] If one accepts the importance of openness to otherness, then one must treat culture as a 'window' not as a 'cell'.[22] It should be a place from which the world can be seen, in all its richness and diversity, not one from which it should be screened off, or whose awkward features are filtered out from study.

Both the capacity to transcend cultural frameworks, called for by Burtonwood, and the breadth of outlook to avoid the defects of monism, against which Parekh warns us, are required for life in a pluralist society that seeks to be democratic, even-handed and rely on a consensus of and a coalition from a diversity of cultures. However, it should be noted that if democracy is 'a culture of criticism and disagreement,'[23] it is also one that rests on some basic, deep-seated and stable agreements. I believe that Catholic schools can and often do function as constitutive communities that provide a foundation and context for the development of basic, deep-seated and stable beliefs and values from which the wider society can benefit. I also believe that those who hold strong non-liberal views, that is, views that are not part of a liberal philosophy, can legitimately resist the suggestion that they cannot cope with or welcome the critical questioning that is part of the democratic consciousness. This suggestion of Burtonwood's is overstated.[24] It is more accurate to say that the relationship between 'a curriculum for cultural attachment and one for democratic citizenship and cross-cultural understanding'[25] will be one of creative tension than to assert that they cannot be reconciled.

My general argument in sections four and five has been that the recognition of increasing pluralism in society and a deeper appreciation of the kind of response required from Christians jointly challenge the Catholic community's self-understanding, its stance towards the world, its relationship with the State and, in particular, both the tone and the detail of its case for Church schooling. It has been shown that the presence of pluralism does pose new challenges to the Church and that some critics of non-liberal worldviews have diagnosed the implications of pluralism for a democratic society more rapidly and more acutely than have religious believers. However, it has also been argued that criticisms of the attempts of faith communities to preserve their traditions, while deserving their careful attention and often adjustments in their practice, do not undermine or destroy the case for a distinctive approach to education. The critical reflection prompted by a greater awareness of pluralism helps faith communities to maintain their honesty, integrity and self-awareness. It could also be argued that some of the qualities developed in their members by faith communities ensure that qualities required for effective citizenship are communicated vividly, developed with both motivation and discipline, internally appropriated and acted upon intelligently.

RECOMMENDED READING

Arthur, J., *The Ebbing Tide* (Leominster: Gracewing, 1995).

Bishops' Conference of England and Wales, *Partners in Mission* (Chelmsford: Matthew James Publishing, 1997).

Congregation for Catholic Education, *The Religious Dimension of Education in a Catholic School* (London: Catholic Truth Society, 1988).

Congregation for Catholic Education, *The Catholic School on the Threshold of the Third Millennium* (Boston: Pauline Books & Media, 1998).

Conroy, J. (ed.), *Catholic Education: Inside Out/Outside In* (Dublin: Lindisfarne/Veritas, 1999), ch. 6.

Eaton, M. (ed.), *Commitment to Diversity* (London: Cassell, 1999).

Groome, T., *Educating for Life* (Allen, Texas: Thomas More Press, 1998).

Lombaerts, H., (trans.) Terry Collins, *The Management and Leadership of Christian Schools* (Groot Bijgaaden, Belgium: Vlaams Lasalliaans Perspectief, 1998).

McBrien, R., *Catholicism* (London: Geoffrey Chapman, 1981), ch. XXX.

NOTES

1. Bernard Lonergan, *Method in Theology* (London: Darton, Longman & Todd, 1972), p. 301. As a philosopher and theologian who taught for many years both in Rome and in North America at major Catholic seminaries and universities, Lonergan has been immensely influential in the transition from a mainly neo-scholastic form of Catholic intellectual endeavour to a more pluralistic, historically critical and hermeneutically sophisticated form of enquiry among Catholic scholars. He was steeped in the conceptual categories and methodology of Aquinas, yet increasingly open to other forms of thought. In chapter four, I offer a more detailed summary of the changes that have taken place in Catholic theology and how these affect our understanding of Catholic education.

2. Ibid., p. 326.

3. See Lonergan, *A Second Collection* (ed.) W. Ryan and B. Tyrrell (London: Darton, Longman & Todd, 1975); *A Third Collection* (ed.) F. E. Crowe (London: Geoffrey Chapman, 1985).

4. Thus it seems that Lonergan went beyond a merely descriptive acknowledgement of plurality. The degree to which pluralism could be recommended, as in some way normative for Christians, is unclear in Lonergan. I think that his work, taken as a whole, can be interpreted as advocating a critical yet open stance in the face of pluralism, a stance that would enable Christians to cope with and to learn from their current pluralist context.

5. John Kekes, *The Morality of Pluralism* (Princeton University Press, 1993), p. 12.

6. Ibid., pp. 19, 29.

7. Ibid., pp. 201-2, the first emphasised by Isaiah Berlin, the second by John Rawls, the third by Ronald Dworkin and the fourth by Joseph Raz.

8. Ibid., pp. 203-4. 'Substantive values are derived from various conceptions of a good life; they are the virtues, ideal, and goods intrinsic to particular conceptions of a good life... Procedural values regulate the pursuit of substantive values by being rules or principles for settling conflicts, distributing resources, protecting people, and setting priorities among substantive values.'

9. Ibid., p. 206.

10. Bishops' Conference of England and Wales, *Catholic Schools and Other Faiths* (London: Catholic Education Service, 1996), demonstrates a very positive interpretation of and response to religious pluralism within society in general and within Catholic schools in particular. Its implementation by teachers and governors probably requires an increase in the level of theological 'literacy' and pastoral sensitivity displayed by many teachers and governors in Catholic schools.

11. T. H. McLaughlin, 'Liberalism, education and the common school', *Journal of Philosophy of Education*, vol. 29, no. 2, July 1995, pp. 239-55, at pp. 241-2. Such an education will exert, according to McLaughlin, both a 'centripetal (unifying) and [a] centrifugal (diversifying) force on pupils and on society'.

12. Amy Gutmann (ed.), *Multiculturalism* by Charles Taylor (Princeton University Press, 1994), p. xi.

13. Deborah Fitzmaurice, (ed.) John Horton, *Liberalism, Multiculturalism and Toleration* (London: Macmillan, 1993), p. 68.

14. Bhikhu Parekh, 'Moral philosophy and its anti-pluralist bias', *Philosophy and Pluralism* (ed.) David Archard (Cambridge University Press, 1996).

15. Ibid., pp. 127-30.

16. Ibid., p. 129. As Parekh says, it 'helps us to appreciate the uniqueness as well as the strengths and limitations of our own [culture], extends our sympathies, deepens our self-knowledge, and enables us to enrich our way of life by borrowing whatever is attractive in others and can be integrated into our own'.

17. Neil Burtonwood, 'Beyond culture: a reply to Mark Halstead', *Journal of Philosophy of Education*, vol. 30, no. 2, 1996, pp. 295-9, at p. 297 (quoting Gupta and Ferguson). As a worldwide religious community, Catholicism is itself thoroughly multicultural and multi-ethnic.

18. Burtonwood, loc. cit. Halstead's article, 'Voluntary apartheid? Problems of schooling for religious and other minorities in democratic societies' is in *Journal of Philosophy of Education*, vol. 29, no. 2, pp. 257-72. Much of Halstead's work, here and elsewhere, takes into account especially the perspectives of Muslim communities living in a secular society.

19. Burtonwood, p. 296.

20. Ibid., p. 297.

21. Ibid., p. 298.

22. Walter Feinberg, 'Liberalism and the aims of multicultural education', *Journal of Philosophy of Education*, vol. 29, no. 2, 1995, pp. 203-16, at p. 204.

23. Michael Walzer, 'Education, democratic citizenship and multiculturalism', *Journal of Philosophy of Education*, vol. 29, no. 2, 1995, pp. 181-9, at p. 186.

24. Burtonwood, loc. cit., p. 298. Also overstated is his suggestion (p. 299) that non-liberal communities will aim for a cosy uniformity and the shunning of all contact with doubt.

25. Ibid.

Chapter Two

School as Family

Almost regardless of the leading purposes aimed for in educational establishments, there is usually a desire on the part of heads/principals that their school should reflect at least some of the features of a family. They hope that, together, the teachers, administrators, ancillary staff and students will comprise a group of people who have much in common, who are willing to share their gifts and talents, who feel safe with one another and who exercise a high degree of care, consideration and mutual support. When schools do display family-like qualities, they offer a welcoming atmosphere, they exhibit a concern for the welfare of their members and they demonstrate a sensitivity to the individuality of each person. They work hard to ensure that all feel accepted, that all have a part to play and that all enjoy a sense of belonging.

Three aspects of the metaphor 'school as family' are explored in this chapter. First, some of the features of family life are described, inviting comparison with life in schools. Through the families from which they draw their students, schools are able to benefit from much valuable 'capital' – human resources and experiences that provide a necessary emotional and social foundation for the enterprise of learning. School leaders are challenged to consider which features of family life either can or indeed should be reflected in an educational community. Second, the family metaphor is extended to include the wider network that often surrounds and enriches our domestic lives. School leaders are invited to question how relevant this notion of extended family is to their own belonging to networks of similar, faith-based schools, and what the implications might be if this notion were taken more seriously. Third, brief consideration is given to some of the expectations that might be appropriate for a Catholic school in developing partnerships with parents. There is a manifest duty to give such partnerships a high priority, if schools are genuinely seeking to implement a Catholic philosophy of education. It is clear, however, that although there are many opportunities to strengthen home-school partnerships, these will not be without tensions and difficulties on both sides.

1. FAMILY 'CAPITAL'

Given the close link between home, Church and school that is an integral part of the Catholic educational partnership, and given the exalted position, with both rights and responsibilities, attributed to parents in the principles governing Catholic education, it would not be surprising if the notion of school as family received added emphasis in that sector. First of all, there is additional 'capital' to draw upon: where the majority of teachers, students and parents share a background in the Catholic faith, there is likely to be a more consistent reinforcing of values held in common. The 'plausibility structure' of home and school will be positively interactive and mutually supportive. Many jointly shared assumptions, priorities and perspectives will be operative in daily decision-making and in the routines of normal life. Furthermore, the scope for partnership between home and school is extended beyond that possible for a secular school, when families and schools each subscribe to the overarching social reality of a Church that embraces and yet simultaneously transcends both.

Of course, it should not be assumed too readily that all family life is benign or, even when it is, that it is experienced as good. The atmosphere in a family can be suffocating, cramped, hostile and demeaning. Abuse, bullying, intolerance, lack of recognition of and respect for individuality can threaten us all the more in a context that persists over many years and for so much of the day, as happens in unhappy families. In circumstances like these, authoritarianism can intrude much further into our lives than in a school; at the same time, there is less room for escape. It is likely that there are more dysfunctional families than dysfunctional schools, since families are less subject to public scrutiny and are called to account to a much lesser degree. Under the cover of privacy, malignant measures have as much scope as beneficial practices. When school is considered under the aspect of 'family', it will be the positive features that I propose to reflect upon.

> Kellmer-Pringle (1975) outlined a fourfold classification of children's needs: the need for love and security; the need for new experiences; the need for praise and recognition; and the need for responsibility. (From Sheila Wolfendale, *Empowering Parents and Teachers* [London: Cassell, 1992], pp. 92-3.)

1. How well do you think these needs are being met in your school?

To what extent can a school aspire to be like a family? There will be some respects in which one might justifiably claim that, the closer a school can reflect the features of family life, the better. There will be other respects in which a school *cannot* reflect family-like features. This might be due to factors such as size, diversity of expectations, external pressures and the constraints of an organisation most of whose members attend by compulsion. Finally, there will be some aspects of family life that a school *should not* seek to replicate; to do so would be to act beyond its mandate and perhaps at the same time to undermine the family itself.

A family usually offers some combination of the following features. First, it is a *mixed-age* and an intergenerational community, with at least two generations, and often more than two, in constant interaction. Even in a nuclear family, the youngest child could easily be mixing with older brothers or sisters who are ten, twelve or more years older. This mixed-age community in itself provides a context for much personal and social learning. The pooling of experience, the first-hand observation of the different interests, strengths and needs of people of different ages, the curiosity and sometimes even delight in the ways of those older and younger than us – all force open the doors of any prison-house of egocentrism with regard to current fads and routines. Here the very young have as much to offer as their elders; their facility to cope with the new, their energy, their wonder and their capacity to dwell fully in the present go some way to compensate for their lack of experience, wisdom and perspective

Second, the family is an *enduring*, long-term community, one that, if not permanent, at least persists over a lengthy period of time. It is also a twenty-four-hour community, in the sense that, although its members may be absent for part of the time, it never 'closes' or 'shuts down'. Although there may be set times and particular routines (for example, at meals), family life, on the whole, is a context where the rule of the clock is less imperious, where there is more scope for flexibility, where a considerable space for open-endedness is allowed as a constituent feature of some activities. Families that appear pressured by 'business', by a concern to be more efficient or to do things quickly, seem to lose some of the advantages and desirable features of home. Home is meant to be a place where we can just *be* together, without a particular goal in mind.

Third, a family, despite the exercise of parental authority through particular explicit rules and unspoken assumptions that hold sway, is, for the most part, an *informal* community. It is also one that allows for a great deal of intimacy, interaction on many fronts, the expression of a wide range of emotions and a massive amount of mutual support. It is a community where practice, custom and habit so override theory or precept as to render them irrelevant or unnecessary. Here hearts and hands have priority over heads. Close proximity, regular touch, constant and unscheduled verbal exchange, mutual accommodation, frequent sharing, rhythms of argument and reconciliation, times of undisguised vulnerability and disappointment punctuated by occasions of elation and celebration – these are all part of the pattern of family life.

Fourth, a family at its best is a place where one feels at home, where one experiences *acceptance*, where one belongs, where one can be relaxed and natural. Here one can express one's feelings, expose one's fears and explore one's dreams. Here one can try out new language, dabble in new interests, even rehearse new personae, without any of these being taken as irrevocable steps or as undermining one's acceptability. Here one is loved, without condition, regardless of achievement. Each member will be recognised for his or her idiosyncrasies, specialness and uniqueness, with a mixture of appreciation and respect, irritation and tolerance, amusement and wonder, but these responses will bear little or no relation to public achievement or worldly success. They will acknowledge, in some implicit way, the mysterious identity and otherness of each individual.

Four positive features of family life have been identified: these might be referred to as (a) their mixed-age/intergenerational nature; (b) the time dimension; (c) their informality and intimacy; and (d) the 'hospitable space' for individuality.

2. To what extent is there room in your school to derive more benefit for students from the first of these features? What activities or arrangements might be considered so as to draw more out of this potential social 'capital'?

3. With regard to (b), do schools unnecessarily rule out certain kinds of possible experiences and achievements through an inflexible use of time? How could current timetable arrangements be 'loosened up' without undermining the main work of the school?

4. Comment on the opportunities for – and limits to – informality and intimacy in school life.

5. Identify the alternative 'goods' or legitimate goals of school that are in some tension with the promotion of individuality. Are there any steps that might be taken to ensure that the balance between these goods and providing a 'hospitable space' for individuality is appropriate and healthy?

6. How do the social circumstances of your students affect their experience and expectations of family life and the kind of pastoral needs they bring to school?

7. What are the arguments for and against visits by teachers to the homes of students, in the pursuit of school 'business'?

Take one of the classes you teach. How would you describe your relationship with each of the students in the class? What information do you have about their academic ability? What personal details do you know? How much time have you spent with them over the past month? What do the answers to these questions tell you about your values and assumptions? (Adapted from David Tuohy, *The Inner World of Teaching* [London, Falmer Press, 1999], p. 23.)

8. One of the features of family life at its best is the degree of trust it facilitates among its members, allowing confidences to be shared without fear of exposure. What are the particular challenges for school leaders with regard to confidentiality (regarding students, staff and families)?

Free human dialogue, wandering wherever the agility of the mind allows, lies at the heart of education. (Neil Postman, *The End of Education* [New York: Vintage, 1996], p. 27).

In the busy world of school life, with constraints of formality, timetabling pressures, the demands of examinations and public testing, and over-full curricula, how in practice do you ensure that there are 'spaces' where such free and 'wandering' dialogue can occur, unscheduled and with spontaneity? Without the apparent 'luxury' of such disconnected and unbidden moments the climate in school can rapidly become over-structured, lifeless and impersonal, and, to that extent, most 'unfamilylike'.

9. What would be the implications for school leadership and management if the promotion of free dialogue were explicitly adopted as a priority? What changes might be needed, for example, in curriculum design, pedagogical styles, student grouping, timetabling, the school environment and accommodation?

2. EXTENDED FAMILIES

One of the features of many nuclear families is that they receive at least part of their identity from belonging to an extended family that includes grandparents, uncles and aunts, cousins, nephews and nieces, in-laws and 'honorary' family members, in addition to girlfriends and boyfriends and all kinds of long-term and temporary partnerships. Gatherings of the wider family, whether for celebration or for grief, add enormously to the richness of family life. Birthdays, anniversaries, sacramental and secular milestones, times of joy and sorrow, all are imprinted on our memory with a special dimension when shared with the extended family. This is where we first learn the rudiments of secular 'liturgy', when we transcend the initial boundaries of home, where we see our closest family members interact with people who are significant others for them. In the process we come to see our own immediate family in a slightly different light. Children see a role-change when their parents are themselves acting as sons or daughters, or when they act more playfully than is customary at home, as uncles or aunts. Young people can experience the benign and non-controlling interest of older family members who, suspended from the requirements of direct responsibility, are allowed the liberty of simply *enjoying* the exploration, the wonder, the foibles and follies of children.

In contexts such as these, there are fresh opportunities for learning the meaning of sharing, for appreciating the diversity of personalities, for re-orienting our understanding of our circumstances because of the new perspective we have gained. Our insight into the relative importance and scope of values and customs is deepened, whether these values and customs are reinforced, contradicted or qualified. A significantly enriched form of modelling of roles and behaviour is possible. At their best, such wider family gatherings will extend our understanding, boost our confidence, stimulate our curiosity and strengthen our bonds.

How might this notion of extended family relate to the school context? First, one might expect that where students have already had substantial experience of the extended family, they will find the transition to school less traumatic and more of a natural step. And vice versa. Is it legitimate or possible for primary schools to inform themselves about family circumstances in order to take remedial action or seek to provide substitute experience if this is lacking?

Second, while problems of size, numbers and space would make it difficult for secondary schools, one might consider the strategy of bringing schools together for certain occasions in order to replicate, at least in some respects, the experience of the extended family. Even if this coming together were restricted to the staff, I believe that there are several potential advantages for schools. Teachers too often work in isolation, with insufficient dialogue with and feedback from fellow teachers. This applies at every level of seniority and in every phase of education. Insufficient awareness of what colleagues are doing in one's own school undermines the coherence and effectiveness of the education offered. This is compounded by lack of familiarity with what teachers in other similar schools are doing, and even more by what happens in a different sector of education.

Many of those benefits from extended family gatherings suggested above could be available to staff from a group of schools. There can be a relativisation of (and fresh insight into) particular 'rules' and customs. It can be demonstrated that seniors in another context have peers and that roles can be differently interpreted and exercised. Values and priorities held in common can be affirmed. Joint endeavour and achievement can be celebrated in grander settings and with a richer repertoire of modes of celebration. Mutual dependence and co-operation can be acknowledged to be necessarily conducive to the health of the 'body' of education as a whole in the face of the complexity of tasks, diversity of expectations, the shortage of resources, and the stress caused by incessant pressure.

10. How *do* the different parts of the Catholic education system complement one another?

11. Are there different implications for leadership, depending on whether your school is owned by a religious order or a diocesan school?

12. What kinds of benefits and support might be offered to a head/principal for being part of a 'family' or system of Church schools? What kinds of responsibility might be implied from her/him as a result of such involvement?

13. Identify as precisely as possible the main issues that would have to be resolved (issues of principle, of 'politics' and of practicalities) if Catholic schools in your area were to be enabled to function more frequently as part of a wider or extended 'family'.

3. HOME-SCHOOL PARTNERSHIP

Drawing on a 1994 report in the USA, Postman points out 'in 1960, only 5 per cent of our children were born to unmarried mothers. In 1990, the figure was 28 per cent. In 1960, 7 per cent of our children under three lived with one parent. In 1990, 27 per cent. In 1960, less than 1 per cent of our children under eighteen experienced the divorce of their parents. In 1990, the figure was almost 50 per cent.' (Postman, 1996, p. 48).

14. How does this picture relate to the lives of students (and staff) in your school? In what way does your school take into account changing social realities and prevailing patterns of family life? To what extent *can* it? To what degree *should* it?

It is seemly to suppose that ushering in the Kingdom of God is work to be shared among many groups, each with its special competence to assist and improve people.... The more one social institution encroaches upon the functions of another, the more it weakens it. ...It is understood [from the field of ecology] that as one system begins to preempt the purposes of another, the functional capacity of both is undermined. If the school, for example, assumes the prerogatives normally exercised by the family, the family loses some of its motivation, authority, and competence to provide what it is designed to do. ...We have already reached a point where people are quite willing to place their children in schools (called, I believe, Day Care centers) at age two, and expect such schools to socialize them, provide them with emotional security, and teach them moral values, discipline, intellectual skills, creativity, good eating and elimination habits, a healthy attitude toward sex, and tolerance for all

people. Aside from the fact that no school can effectively
do all this, what is left for the children's parents to do?
Perhaps only to decide which school to send their
children to. (Postman, 1979, pp. 107-8).

**15. How confident are you that, in the questions posed and
in the activities undertaken at school, the roles, rights and
responsibilities of the family are not being intruded upon?
What are the occasions or points of tension in this area?
What helps and what hinders their satisfactory resolution?**

Some teachers' hostile and negative attitudes [towards
parental involvement in school] are explicable and
grounded in a number of legitimate concerns, chief
among which are:

- that parents in the classroom will undermine teachers'
  professionalism;
- that parents' views are not necessarily well informed
  and therefore a clash with teachers may be inevitable;
- that the active parents are a vocal, self-selecting group
  who are not representative of all parents.
  (Wolfendale, 1992, pp. 10-11.)

**16. How would you summarise the suspicions or fears of
teachers in your school regarding parent contacts and
involvement?**

Fostering parental involvement in schools will provide benefits by:

- giving children a more effective learning environment, made possible through an increased adult:pupil ratio;
- providing schools with extra personnel and human resources;
- giving parents new insights and understanding about their children, as they build bridges between home learning and school learning;
- providing schools with parents who are knowledgeable about school needs.

[Research shows:]

- Parents have expertise in commenting on development.
- Parents' intimate knowledge of their children can be described by them.
- Parental information can complement professional information.
- The information can show up differing behaviour in different settings.
- The information can serve to highlight concerns regarding progress.
- Parents can provide a realistic appraisal of their children. (Wolfendale, 1992, pp. 57, 80.)

In its guidelines for reflection and renewal, *The Religious Dimension of Education in a Catholic School* (Rome, 1988), the

Congregation for Catholic Education advocates a family atmosphere in school, one where students can feel 'at home' (28). Ideally, there will be rooms for parent-teacher meetings (28). In some cases the presence of members of religious communities will bring a special dimension to the family and community ethos (35). 'Close cooperation with the family is especially important when treating sensitive issues such as religious, moral, or sexual education, orientation toward a profession, or a choice of one's vocation in, life' (42). Interestingly, despite reiterating the traditional teaching that 'the first and primary educators of children are their parents' and that 'God has bestowed on the family its own specific and unique educational mission', the Congregation points out that parents are not always sufficiently aware of their duties, and says: 'it is the school's responsibility to give them this awareness. Every school should initiate meetings and other programmes which will make the parents more conscious of their role, and help to establish a partnership; it is impossible to do too much along these lines' (43). Two of the twelve unfavourable conditions listed for Catholic schools refer to the family: 'relationships with families are formal or even strained; and families are not involved in helping to determine the educational goals' (104).

17. Are there times when a strict and clear separation of home and school is in the best interests of any or all parties?

18. Apart from the possibility of a designated room, what practical factors or arrangements have a bearing on effective and confident meetings between teachers and parents?

19. What, in your experience, have been the sensitive areas/issues in school relationships with families and

parents? What most helps the constructive resolution of such concerns?

20. In your assessment of the degree to which your school displays 'familylike' features, and the level of awareness of their responsibilities shown by families that send students to your school, where should efforts be directed next? Should attention focus more on (a) modifying structures and strategies in the school or (b) modifying parental levels of awareness and patterns of behaviour?

There are many different levels of parental involvement in school life. These include: being kept informed, being invited to observe what goes on, being invited to comment on policies and practices, contributing to the teaching and learning life of the school, being consulted on decision-making and even sharing in the governance of the school. Many parents want only a minimal role. Relevant factors here might be their memories of school, their level of education and their lack of affinity with the Church. Other factors might be a high level of satisfaction with or trust in the school, their other preoccupations, responsibilities and concerns, their state of health, their economic circumstances, in addition to their beliefs, values and expectations concerning school. Other parents desire a much fuller role. This may be an expression of commitment to their children, or a desire for partnership with the school, or perhaps a lack of complete trust in the school. It may be due to the fact that they are confident about the educational world, familiar with its language and committed to its standards and requirements. Perhaps they envisage involvement in school life as an aspect of citizenship or as part of what is entailed by being an active member of the Church.

21. Review the different levels of parental involvement in the life of your school and indicate which factors you believe have been most influential in arriving at this pattern. Are there steps that the school management might take in addressing this situation?

22. How does the Church dimension influence home-school relationships and mutual expectations? For whom and over what issues is the Church a complication, an obstacle or a positive resource in home-school relations?

In this chapter, consideration has been given to the notion of school as a family and also to the management of relationships between schools and families. While there are certainly valuable benefits to be gained if schools seek to reflect features of family life in their daily work, it is clear that there will be both jurisdictional and practical limitations to this attempt. At the same time, while sound and positive relationships between school and home should be a priority for school leaders, it is only one of many such priorities, and the energies of staff in this area have to be balanced out by attention to other aspects of school business. If students are to benefit from the mutual respect, real understanding and due appreciation that should be shown between schools and families, there is a demanding and continuing agenda for school leaders.

In addition to the usual issues of partnership and areas of concern between school and families, in the context of Catholic schools there are other duties for school leaders. They must talk about the mission of the school with parents, recognise and support them as the primary educators of their children in the faith and enable pupils to contribute to the local and wider Church. In return, parents should be invited to help the staff to understand better what pupils really need and also to support the school in its task of moral and spiritual formation. When teachers and parents acknowledge in each other an equivalent (although different) expertise, a share in collective responsibility and the need for reciprocal reporting as positive features of home-school relations[2] (Wolfendale, *Empowering Parents and Teachers* [London: Cassell, 1992], pp. 92-3.) a sound foundation for effective communication will have been provided. Then they will be well placed to explore openly together what they want and need from each other, what is helping and hindering this and how they can co-operate better together.

RECOMMENDED READING

Bradford, J., *Caring for the Whole Child* (London: The Children's Society, 1995).

Collins, U. and McNiff, J., *Rethinking Pastoral Care* (London: Routledge, 1999).

Feheney, M., (ed.) *Education and the Family* (Dublin: Veritas, 1995).

—— *From Ideal to Action* (Dublin: Veritas, 1998), ch. 6.

Monahan, L., *Making School A Better Place* (Dublin: Marino Institute of Education, 1996).

Treston, K., *Choosing Life. Pastoral Care for School Communities* (Brisbane: Creation Enterprises, 1997).

Wolfendale, S., *Empowering Parents and Teachers* (London: Cassell, 1992).

CHAPTER THREE

SCHOOL AS BUSINESS

In chapter two it became clear that although there are many respects in which it is legitimate to think of school as a place that reflects the positive features of family life, there are also limits to the use of the family metaphor. These limits are due to the contrasting nature, scale, purpose and circumstances of family, as compared with school. Both *de facto* and *de jure*, the respective roles of school and family are different. In the same way, it will be claimed here that there is some value in viewing school as a business, but also that there are limits to the appropriateness of using this metaphor. Such an approach, if pursued without discernment, is likely to distort the true nature of school communities and to undermine essential features of educational relationships.

In this chapter, five aspects of what might be entailed by treating school as a business are considered. First, and very briefly, I pick out two positive features of business practice – strategic planning and customer service – and I suggest that both of these can enhance the work of Catholic schools. Second, the scope of resource management in the school context is examined. Third, I indicate some of the challenges presented by recent emphases on the role of market forces in education. Fourth, since the notion of school as a business draws upon assumptions about the nature of work and its function in our lives, I bring these into focus in such a way as to bring out the need for a spirituality of work. Fifth, some of the shortcomings of 'managerialism' in education are explored.

1. STRATEGIC PLANNING AND CUSTOMER SERVICE

When school is considered as a 'business', several features of its management and functioning come to the fore. I comment briefly on just two of these features here. First, there is the notion of *strategic planning*. This embraces an audit of current strengths and weaknesses, a mapping of internal and external threats and opportunities, prioritising from the many claims made upon the institution for a diverse range of 'services' or products, identifying the core mission of the business, and drawing up a vision of what the organisation (and its constituent parts) will look like in the foreseeable future. Then targets and action plans to address agreed priorities must be specified, along with associated resource implications, timescales, support and monitoring arrangements and indicators of successful performance.

Such strategic planning is intended to move a school from pious rhetoric about ideals to real improvement. It can include consultation, scanning the environment, considering alternatives, ensuring coherence among priorities and co-ordination of effort. Above all, it offers a sense of direction and a degree of control over change. All schools can surely benefit from this kind of strategic planning.

A second key element in a businesslike approach is taking seriously the notion of *customer service*. Rather than schools exercising a monopoly over education, thereby considering students and parents as captive audiences, customer service acknowledges the choices available to people to secure the 'goods' of education elsewhere and sets out to satisfy and retain present 'customers' and to attract more of them. Students and parents are treated as stakeholders or shareholders in the educational enterprise, with rights to information and consultation, and with opportunities for feedback on the degree to which their expectations are being met. As valued customers, they are invited to influence the school's priorities and policies.

The notion of 'internal customer' also emphasises the interdependence of the work carried out by different groups within the school, for example, teachers and support staff. One cannot be fully effective in isolation, for each member of staff depends upon all the others to carry out their responsibilities appropriately, as they, in turn, depend upon us to do our part. In this way, customer service implies mutual respect, awareness of the needs of others and at least an overview of the structure of the 'business' as a whole, so that its functioning can be understood.

Customer service ensures that notions like efficiency, economy, quality and infrastructure are brought into close relation with the perspectives, needs, hopes and frustrations of the people involved, and especially the people we are there to serve. It prevents people from being taken for granted and it aims to change the emphasis from envisaging school as a compulsory institution, with 'inmates' to be kept in line, to one where a desirable product is made attractive and where consent is readily granted. It seeks to boost levels of satisfaction, it takes complaints seriously and it aims to work strenuously at ensuring that positive attitudes towards the school are held by those who work there and those who come to receive a service. 'This is *your* school; how can we make it serve you better?', is the dominant attitude when a customer-service orientation is adopted, rather than 'fit in or get out!' The notion of customer service is surely one that harmonises well with the purposes of Christian schooling.

1. Before proceeding further, what kind of 'business' do you envisage your school more closely resembling: a little, local corner shop, a large supermarket or an exclusive and specialised store?

2. RESOURCE MANAGEMENT

There is, of course, a duty on the staff in a school to dispose of resources made available from public funds – or indeed from private funds – and, in doing so, to act prudently and responsibly. First, resources are always finite, usually insufficient to match our aspirations, and a decision to deploy them in one way often rules out alternative strategies. In this sense it is crucial to avoid waste. Second, since the money is not our own, we are expected to act as stewards in its allocation, directing its use to serve the purposes for which the school was founded and its current priorities. Third, since money and resources are, like knowledge and information, sources of power and influence in a community, they are open to abuse, either in their ready provision or by selective withholding. School leaders must not only avoid temptations to show favouritism to those who comply with their wishes or to punish or pressurise those who fail to do so; they must also be careful not to lay themselves open to such perceptions, thereby undermining staff morale. The 'economic' aspects of school inescapably have a moral dimension.

The allocation of resources, including remuneration, accommodation, learning resources, time and professional development opportunities, should recognisably display several features. First, it should be transparent rather than hidden. Such openness brings decisions about resources out of the shadows and into the light. It helps in reducing rumour, misunderstanding and inaccurate guesswork. By being better informed about the basis of resource allocation decisions, staff usually feel more empowered to contribute to the sometimes painful decisions that have to be made and more willing to act upon them. If they are left in the dark and expected to show blind trust, then responsible ownership of school decisions is made almost impossible for them.

Second, the allocation of resources must be justifiable in terms of meeting public and objective criteria, rather than being carried out on a whim, or as personal patronage, or because of the strength of the school leader's feeling towards a particular priority, or as a result of pressure from one quarter or another within (or external to) the school. Inevitably, because of the principal's overview of the school and access to information from many sources, some of which are confidential, he or she will have a depth of understanding – of both internal and external factors – that is not readily available to others. But if decisions about giving out the 'goods' of the school are to be de-personalised, made more objective and warranted by public criteria, then one of the tasks of school leadership will be that of educating staff (as well as others) about the relevant factors, their bearing on the budget, etc., and how they impact upon each other. In this way the third criterion for distribution of the school's resources, equitability, has a chance to become operative. It is important that staff believe that resource decisions are just, that nobody is excluded and that nobody is unfairly advantaged. For this, a careful assessment is needed of how to balance out the respective roles and duties of each with the needs related to these roles. An accurate overview must be reached as to how each of the parts relate to the whole school enterprise.

Thus it is incumbent on school leaders to 'cut the cake' – the whole range of resources – in such a way that the main priorities of the school are transparently being addressed. In business terms, the staff are the central resource, the main 'plant' that must be maintained. This does not mean, however, that the overriding priority in allocating the budget must be the retention of all staff currently on the payroll. School is not an employment agency. Staff are employed in order to assist the school in its overriding task of providing students with a quality education. For this purpose, the students also need a safe, healthy and warm building, accommodation that facilitates learning, appropriate resources, and so on. Therefore, a principal or head must ensure that staff salaries do not so dominate the budget that other necessities for student learning are neglected.

The task of balancing the budget, of ensuring adequate remuneration for staff and the just rewarding of effort and responsibility, at the same time as meeting the requirements of students for resources other than teachers, is complex. It demands powers of insight and judgement and qualities of compassion and courage. Account has to be taken of the multiple and differing (sometimes diametrically opposed) perceptions of people within and beyond the school. Decisions must not only be guided by principles and values, they must also be rooted in accurate assessment of the relevant economic and educational realities facing the school, to facilitate the best possible use of limited resources. Sensitivity to the needs of the marginalised, disempowered, weaker members of the school community, those who do not have strong advocates, those most in need of support, must be shown. All should feel that they count, that they matter, that they are taken notice of and that they can make a difference by offering a valued contribution. The 'antennae' of the principal should be highly developed so that she or he can hear the voices that are muffled or submerged by the school's dominant contenders. The capacity to detect this aspect of the school culture is as necessary as the ability to scan the school's external environment. At the same time, a high degree of moral courage is needed to carry through resource decisions that uphold the school's major purposes and values in the face of opposition or unpopularity, or when tempted by alternative and unworthy short-cuts.

If the 'business' dimension of school is to be run efficiently, staff need to be encouraged to cost priorities and projects that they wish to espouse and to be aware of the resource implications of their current practice. For example, do they know the typical or average cost of lessons given to students in year four, in year eight or twelve? Can they be helped to see that knowing the answer to this question may be relevant not only to the school's prudent management of its resources but also to its educational effectiveness? They may well need some assistance in taking into account the various factors that must be included in arriving at any estimate of the cost of current practice, for example, percentage of salary in relation to time spent, and allowance for contribution to heating, lighting, accommodation and running costs, as well as the possible cost of not doing something else. Alternative strategies or new proposals must be related to current and projected costs and available resources, in addition to their relative priority in the educational purposes of the school.

Making the best of what we have is a moral, as well as an economic imperative. To this end, the hoarding (and associated minimal use) of resources must be prevented, care should be taken with equipment so that unnecessary repair bills are avoided and proposals for expenditure should be justified with as much professionalism as planning student learning experiences. Too often, resources are purchased without adequate justification, then lie unused in cupboards, thereby reducing the budget for necessities. Staff should identify how proposals for new purchases relate to intended learning outcomes, and for whom. A record needs to be kept identifying the location of (and the person responsible for) different resources, their designated age-group, and some indication of current usage, including reference to frequency and impact. Did they turn out to be as useful as expected? Is the right balance or range of resources being planned for over a period of time?

Many management decisions, including those related to the economic, business and resource dimensions, can only be properly understood and implemented in the light of a long-term development plan. Such planning cannot, without damage to the principle of subsidiarity, and therefore without undermining local responsibility, be taken only at the level of the head or principal. Resource plans must take into account, be supportive of, indeed be integrated into, the educational planning of teachers at classroom level.

2. (a) In your school, how are the following aspects of resource management dealt with and by whom?

(i)   *purchase* (fit with schemes of work; capacity to enhance teaching and learning styles; appropriateness for ages/abilities of students; considering alternatives/making comparisons; guidance about use);

(ii)   *access* (storage; labelling; information about; system for use);

(iii)   *monitoring* (wear and tear; rate of loss; continuing appropriateness for course/students; effectiveness/response achieved; satisfaction level of students and staff);

(iv)   *liaison*

- *with special educational needs provision* (schemes of work; learning needs; support staff; evaluation of appropriateness of resources);
- *with information and communication technology provision* (staff confidence; access to equipment; availability of materials/software; collaboration with other sections of the school);

- *with library* (schemes of work and curriculum planning; joint discussion about resources; study-skills co-operation; timing, nature and requirements of key assignments/projects).

(b) Are there any aspects of good practice in resource management that deserve to be acknowledged and disseminated further, and are there any weaknesses that require intervention?

Consider the following scenario:

With the introduction of *Local Financial Management of Schools* the school finance committee has to make some difficult decisions about priorities. In the context of falling student rolls, intense competition from other schools, plus a reduced budget, hard-headed realism is needed about the ability to attract more students to ensure the very survival as well as the success of the school.

A. It is decided that, in order to attract the right kind of interest among parents and to draw the right kind of positive publicity from the local press, special financial support will be given to two areas of the curriculum, Latin and Media Studies, in the next three years. Regrettably, this will have to be at the expense of a reduced allocation to Special Needs, to Physical Education (PE) and to Personal and Social Education (PSE). With regard to the first of these, only twelve students regularly received help last year; the view was taken that the school could not let so small a number of students affect the fate of the whole school. With regard to the second, the Secretary of State for Education seems to be hinting that outside school hours, sporting activities can count as PE. With regard to the third subject adversely affected, many staff feel ill-prepared for PSE anyway and believe that it is lightweight and unnecessary.

B. It is also decided that since Mr Picasso is so useless an Art teacher, always getting very poor results in examinations, and that by slightly increasing the number in all Art classes the school can manage without him, he will be made redundant by the governing body. The money saved will be spent on hiring a recently retired expert on marketing, in order to boost recruitment to the school. It is well known that there are only enough children in the primary schools in the area to support one secondary school. This school will ensure that it is not at risk of decline or closure.

What is your considered response to A and B?

There has been widespread delegation of financial and other aspects of resource management responsibility down to school level. Often this move serves simultaneously to reduce the scope of local area authorities and to enhance the power of the State to influence educational developments. There are many factors operating here, including the inexorable and exponential increase in expenditure on education (and other social services), and the strong desire on the part of governments to bring this spending under close scrutiny and more effective control. One means of achieving this has been to add financial management responsibilities to those other leadership duties already exercised by heads and principals in the spheres of curriculum, professionalism, community-building, and, in the case of faith-based schools, religion, spiritual formation and development. There has been a mixed response from school leaders to the imposition of, or, depending on one's theoretical perspective and experience 'on the ground', the opportunity afforded by, financial management. This is itself related to beliefs and expectations, within and beyond the school, about the degree to which schools should reflect external social and economic realities, be kept separate from them, or even perhaps have a role that calls them into question.

3. MARKET FORCES

Among the major attitudinal changes in the context affecting schools, we may note a widespread expectation that closer links will be established between, on the one hand, the priorities and emphases within the curriculum and, on the other, the economic needs of the country and the particular skills required by employers. If in a former age, school often functioned as a clearly protected, relatively pure sphere, one that delayed introduction to the rather dirtier world of industry, commerce and sharp-edged competition, this is no longer seen as an adequate preparation for life. The academic curriculum not only remained inaccessible to many students, but what was worse in the view of politicians, it developed qualities and skills that did not easily transfer to the 'real' world outside. As a result, many experiments have been introduced into schools in the last twenty years to bring to the fore a focus on the world of work, vocational studies, careers guidance, opportunities for enterprise, placements at work and links with further education establishments.

> Education is explicitly justified in terms of how well it can contribute to wealth-creation, useful production, and the

development of talents desired by employers. ... Education is now being required to give a public account of itself as either an item of consumption for which an economic cost has to be paid, or an investment from which an economic return can be derived. ...A highly instrumental view of the world [is encouraged]. ...Education is subordinated to the market economy, and the notion of vocation [is treated] as a response to the market rather than a 'calling' from within. ... [Referring to the UK in the period 1988-89:] Of £214m additional funds allocated to teacher in-service training, £1.1m was earmarked for religious education. [With regard to curriculum priorities] short shrift is given to personal qualities, (except) self-reliance, self-discipline, an enterprising approach and the ability to solve practical real-world problems. There is no philosophical enquiry and no concern with motivational issues. The implication is that in the real world individuality is suspect, conformity is rewarded, and morals are guided by enterprise. ...[There is little] serious acknowledgement of non-monetary values in education – (compassion, trust, sharing and love) rather than usefulness, possession, monetary value and self-interest. ... [We are in a time] when the useful is preferred to the good, the measurable to the unique, the marketable to the fulfilling, and the technological to the moral and spiritual. (Dudley Plunkett, *Secular and Spiritual Values* [London: Routledge, 1990], pp. 20, 27, 28, 31, 37, 39, 43.)

4. What has been your experience of the effects, on education in general and on school leaders in particular, of attempts to make schools more aware of external economic

realities, more responsive to the economic needs of the nation and more accountable for value for money in their own deployment of resources? Has Plunkett overstated his case?

5. To what extent do you think that the role of head/principal as a 'business manager' is likely to affect the 'family' and 'Church' dimensions of Catholic school life and leadership (including the notion of 'extended family')? Is it more of a blessing or a curse?

6. How might the Church as a whole, particularly at both parish and diocesan level, benefit and learn from the school experience of accepting greater responsibility for economic and 'business' matters?

The introduction of or, perhaps more accurately, a more explicit level of State support for, the operation of market principles in education by many governments in the second half of the 1980s, was intended to enhance the opportunity for choice by parents, to reduce the power of professional providers, to minimise passivity and a dependency culture among the public in education as in other spheres of life, and to contribute towards raising quality through more open competition. Behind the market mentality, however, there lurked several assumptions that were neither congenial to educational practice nor conducive to an appreciation of the kind of 'good' that education is. An atomistic view of individuals, a materialist reading of the goal of life, a consumer approach to citizenship, a focus on the exercise of autonomy without due attention to the conditions required for its formation and development – when combined – threaten to turn education into a commodity, to undermine collective action, and to cause us to fail to understand how the private relates to the public in life and how individual choices cumulatively impact on the social fabric.

The avowed rationale for deregulation is that the competitive ethos created by market conditions will shake up a service hidebound by tradition, wrest control from the vested interests of professionals and bureaucrats, and promote more rapid response to the needs of society, understood primarily as an economic entity requiring particular skills and dispositions. ...The nub of the question is whether freedoms to exercise consumer choice in the schooling context are in fact private liberties whose exercise concerns only the chooser, or are social freedoms whose impact on others is either contingently or logically inescapable. ...[W]e have each to be concerned not just with our individual choices but also with the social matrix which makes them the choices that they are. ...[W]hen the concept of citizen as individual consumer is extended to the one social practice [education] which provides the site for the formation of preferences as well as for their satisfaction, this results in a fragmentation of interest and action which denies the public that most basic social good of all; some shared notion of what the good of society consists in. Far from placing us in greater control of our fate, this individualised conception of citizenship simply releases each of us individually to obtain the best deal that we can within the circumstances we have ceased to try and optimise together. ...When we focus on those public benefits which are sought from public education – social cohesion, cultural richness, economic prosperity – we see that at least the first two of these are placed in jeopardy by policies which license, indeed encourage, a scramble for immediate personal interest.[2] (Ruth Jonathan, *Illusory Freedoms: Liberalism, Education and the Market* [Oxford: Blackwell, 1997], pp. 31, 95, 188, 198, 199.)

7. How do these comments on the potential social effects of an emphasis on market forces, when applied to education, relate to your own observations and experience?

4. THE NATURE OF WORK

Behind much of the language about the application of business principles to the sphere of education, there are hidden assumptions about the nature of work and its role in our lives. A critical engagement with business and management thinking, if it is to be founded on Christian principles, should relate our understanding of work to an appreciation of our spiritual nature.

The basis for determining the value of human work is not primarily the kind of work being done but the fact that the one who is doing it is a person. …[W]ork is 'for man' and not man 'for work'. [T]hrough work man *not only transforms nature*, adapting it to his own needs, but he also *achieves fulfilment* as a human being and indeed, in a sense, becomes 'more a human being.' …Working at any workbench, whether a relatively primitive or an ultramodern one, a man can easily see that *through his work he enters into two inheritances*: the inheritance of what is given to the whole of humanity in the resources of nature, and the inheritance of what others have already developed on the basis of those resources, primarily by developing technology. ...In working, man enters into the labours of others. ...[The Church] sees it as her particular duty to *form a spirituality of work* which will help all people to come closer, through work, to God, the Creator and Redeemer, to participate in His salvific plan for man and the world and to deepen their friendship with Christ in their lives by accepting, through faith, a living participation in His three-fold mission as Priest, Prophet and King. ...Man, created in the image of God, *shares by his work* in the activity of the Creator. ...The Christian finds in human work a small part of the Cross of Christ and accepts it in the same spirit of redemption in which Christ accepted His cross for us. (Pope John Paul II, *Laborem Exercens [On Human Work]* [Boston: Pauline Books, 1981], pp. 16-17, 23, 31, 56-7.)

These passages seem to suggest several key priorities as necessary elements in a Christian stance towards work. First, the inalienable dignity of workers is always to be respected and preserved. No matter how efficient or not they may be, and no matter whether their position within an organisation is high or low, they must never be reduced to the level of an object or tool in the hands of those in control or those who own the means of production.

Second, every effort should be made to ensure that work does not degrade or damage human beings. No matter how profitable a form of work appears to be, and despite any positive benefits that seem to accrue to others as its fruits, the well-being of workers is paramount and always has priority over these possible benefits, except in so far as on a clearly voluntary basis workers put themselves forward to go the extra mile out of a sense of a particular vocation or deeply felt commitment to a project.

Third, it is not only legitimate, but also imperative, for those in positions of responsibility at work, to go beyond consideration of issues of efficiency, effectiveness, economy and quality, and to demonstrate a concern for the effect of the work on the workers themselves. If apparent success by the school, for example, in terms of examination results, reputation, position in comparative 'league tables', numbers of pupil applications for places, and so on were 'bought' at the expense of harm to staff health, increased stress, breakdown, damaged relationships or the undermining of family life because of the excessively high level of demands of work, this would be a sign of something so seriously wrong that it would merit urgent attention by those in leadership, oversight or stewardship positions with regard to the school. How extensive this concern should be is obviously a matter for prudent judgement. It is also important to avoid intruding upon privacy and to leave scope for personal responsibility. If the principle of subsidiarity is to be upheld, individuals and their families must have room for initiative, decision-making and the setting of priorities with regard to the balance of pressures and rewards they find worthwhile and manageable.

Fourth, it seems to follow from this concern about the effects of the work on the worker, that those responsible for staff development should interpret this task in broad terms if they are to reflect a catholic approach. If the management team in school focus solely on current priorities for institutional development as their overriding and all-consuming source for planning staff development, they are likely to omit key dimensions of both professional and personal growth and to substitute short-term gains for long-term advances.

Fifth, an understanding of the nature of work, according to the perspective offered by the Pope, implies several things at once. We should take due account of the social dimension of the world of work and the need for collaboration with others. We should reflect on the methods, tools and technology at our disposal, reviewing their effects on ourselves and on others. We should display a respect for creation as God's work of art and as an arena pregnant with God's presence. We should also demonstrate an appreciation of living tradition, from which we borrow and to which we contribute.

Sixth, John Paul II reminds us that it is the Christian's duty to develop a spirituality of work, whereby this aspect of life is properly integrated, through head, heart and hand, into our relationship with and understanding of Jesus the Christ as the Way, the Truth and the Life for us. In the context of a Christian school, it is incumbent on those with leadership responsibilities to facilitate the development of such a spirituality of work among both students and staff. This must be done without compulsion, for the life of the spirit does not flourish without a free and willing heart and without a confident sense of real freedom. But it must evidently be treated as a priority by Christian school leaders, for their spiritual leadership role, while building upon their role as curriculum, professional and community leaders, goes beyond these and indeed should be a distinguishing feature of their purpose for and style of school leadership. This theme will be explored further in chapter six.

Six aspects of papal teaching on work have been picked out for comment: (1) the need to protect and promote the dignity of workers; (2) ensuring that a focus on effectiveness and efficiency is combined with a sensitivity to the well-being of staff; (3) reflecting on and responding to the effects of the work on the workers; (4) implications for staff development; (5) relating work to our social nature, to creation and to tradition; and (6) the need for a spirituality of work.

8. In reflecting on how these six aspects relate to your own school: a) in which area(s) is the school already doing quite well? (b) in which aspect(s) is there a need for further development?

[i] Your life's work is the work you were born to do – the most appropriate vehicle through which to express your unique talents and abilities. ...[ii] The world's great spiritual and philosophical traditions have long recognized the central role that vocational choice plays in the total health and happiness of the individual and in the vitality and character of a culture. ...[iii] We have become fixated on the economic value of work to the exclusion of virtually all other values. ...[iv] Aristotle said, 'Where your talents and the needs of the world cross, there lies your vocation.' ...[v] The elements of *integrity* and *enjoyment* reflect your individual character, your innate interests and talents. The elements of *service* and *excellence* reflect your social nature, your compassion and desire to share with others your highest quality of work. ...[vi] Since it occupies so much of our time, energy and attention, and is so critical to our sense of psychological well-being and social fulfilment, the quality of our work experience deeply affects other areas of our lives. ...[vii] [quoting Albert Schweitzer:] *The only ones among you who will be really happy are those who have sought and found how to serve.* ...[viii] [quoting Jose Ortega y Gasset :] *Human life, by its very nature, has to be dedicated to something.* ... [ix] The work that you truly love to do is the work you were born to do, will be your greatest contribution to others, and will demand the very best from you. ...[x] The new (information) economy

favours people with qualities like self-motivation, initiative, flexibility, ability to work with a team, and the capacity to learn and adapt to change. ...[xi] Talents are not chosen, but recognized. They cannot be learned, but they can and should be developed. ...[xii] To allow yourself to settle for less than your best is to decide to spend your life hounded and haunted by the ghost of might-have-been. ...[xiii] The only ones who can inspire you to excellence are those who are themselves committed to it. (Laurence Boldt, *How to Find the Work you Love* [New York: Penguin, Arkana, 1996], pp. 3-6, 66, 10, 12, 14, 60, 29, 97, 114, 126.)

9. Which of these thirteen short extracts from Boldt do you find helpful and relevant personally or professionally, and which do you find obscure, unrealistic or unhelpful?

Among the many exercises for personal reflection suggested by Boldt, I pick out two (from pp. 78 and 128 respectively) as being of particular relevance to those thinking about the nature of their work in the context of a Christian school:

1. (a) Imagine that you've been told you have five years left to live. In terms of your work life, what is it that you most want to accomplish in your remaining years?

(b) Imagine yourself on your deathbed, filled with regret, with a painful sense of having missed your life's calling. What is it that you most regret not accomplishing?

2. Do you have any 'soft enemies' – people who appear supportive, but tend to encourage limited views of yourself? How can you better protect yourself from these negative influences?

Flexibility is the mantra of the new 'dynamic capitalism'. If you can't cope with change, you don't have a future. …What is corroded by modern capitalism are things like the experience of trust, which is a fundamental commitment – whether you feel you can be trusted, whether you can trust the people you work with and so on. If you have very short-term, superficial relations with people, you're never going to develop trust. Short-term capitalism (the world of downsizing, company 're-engineering', teamwork, and short contracts) threatens to corrode character, particularly those qualities of character which bind human beings to one another and furnishes each with a sense of sustainable self. By character I mean the capacity of someone to sustain for a long period of time a set of purposes and aims that they realise through their own actions. It doesn't take people in flexible companies long to realise that being loyal doesn't pay. Repeated downsizings produce 'lower profits and declining worker productivity'. Who works well if they think they could be next to be shown the door? (Desmond Grady, *The Guardian*, 5 November 1998, p. 8., reporting on Richard Sennett's book *The Corrosion of Character: The Personal Consequences of Work in the New Capitalism*, Norton, 1998.)

10. How relevant to teachers and to school leaders is Sennett's thesis that certain features of current work patterns undermine important aspects of human growth and community life?

11. In the management of change: (a) is sufficient attention given to what should stay the same, to the affirmation of what has worked well, and to those values that must be retained? (b) are those who resist seen merely as obstructive or as possibly offering a discerning defence of the good as they see it? (c) when new priorities and additional tasks are identified as necessary, is sufficient care taken to explore the possibility of stopping, slowing down or reducing the scale or frequency of work devoted to previous priorities and tasks?

In the context of institutions that espouse Christian principles, we should endeavour to promote attitudes to work that harmonise with and nurture a life that is well-rounded, balanced, positive, healthy and creative. Among the implications of such a stance, we might note the following:

- the needs of the 'system' at work should be sensitively related to and balanced by the personal worlds and needs of staff and students;
- a wider and deeper sense of 'vocational' must be fostered;
- the contemplative as well as the active dimension of life needs attention;
- measurement – of all kinds – is less important than relationship;
- authority structures and hierarchy should always be treated as less important than (and in fact in service of) our common discipleship.

5. MANAGERIALISM IN EDUCATION

Sound management benefits both students and staff; the lack of
it causes all 'players' in the 'game' of education to suffer. It
undermines parental confidence in schools and erodes public
sympathy for and appreciation of what goes on in them.
Evidence from inspection suggests that a significant minority of
schools display standards of management that leave something
to be desired. But the managerial imperative that seems to have
swept over schools in many countries in recent years has opened
the way for some abuses, which I label 'managerialism'.

In the promotion of management language, tasks and
culture, and the marginalisation of pedagogy, subject and
professional collegiality, teaching becomes a technology
that can be observed, deconstructed, analysed, costed,
measured and packaged. ...The practitioner and
educational institution are now in receipt of the goals and
values determined elsewhere from the market, or from
external agencies such as [in the case of England] the
School Curriculum and Assessment Authority, the
Teacher Training Agency, the Office for Standards in
Education and the Further Education Funding Council.
...As teachers comply with the national curriculum, test
their pupils, accept appraisal, as heads sit on sub-
committees of governing bodies to apportion the school's
budget, they come gradually to live and be imbued by the
logic of new roles, new tasks, new functions, and, in the
end to absorb partial re-definitions of their professional
selves. ...What the rapid adoption of the managerial
model has done is to exclude other versions of
organisation life from teacher training and development.
...Professional judgement and standards have been

questioned by the adoption of external criteria in assessment and the marginalization of the teacher in relation to the curriculum. Therefore, children's work is determined by efficiency rather than welfare, and they are tested according to a timetable rather than readiness and capability. (Helen Gunter, *Rethinking Education* [London, Cassell, 1997], pp. viii, 9, 10, 14, 15.)

12. To what extent does this complaint, that managerialism in education has resulted in the de-professionalisation of teaching, match the reality of your own national context and local circumstances?

13. How can the introduction of new approaches to management within schools and greater co-ordination of the education service take place without leading to the negative results suggested by Gunter?

Relevance and quality are defined by the person or institution who pays the invoice. ...Teachers have always been interested in outcomes, but not the ones which are measured in league tables. Teachers have always had a sense of accountability, but they question the current emphasis on leaving a paper trail of proformas and policy documents to prove that they are. (Gunter, 1997, p. 48, 97.)

14. How would you describe and explain changes of emphasis in the use of (and response to) words like 'quality' and 'accountability' in education?

Among the assumptions that seem to underpin much recent managerialism in education, Gunter identifies the following:

- management must act, perform, make it happen and have a right to manage disconnected from the social and economic context;
- management is separate in language, form, and function from teaching;
- education has been defined according to economic indicators, and therefore social development and innovation are connected with efficiency and effectiveness rather than equity, justice and liberty;
- efficiency and effectiveness of learning is directly linked with the innovation and application of technology (databases, spreadsheets, e-mail, etc.) in relation to information gathering and dissemination;
- teachers have to be controlled through management techniques by teams, vision and mission, and corporate collaboration. (Gunter, 1997, p. 105.)

15. How does the external (economic and social) context of schools influence the purpose and style of management adopted within them?

16. To what extent does the 'business' of school management require different skills and qualities from that of teaching? How much overlap is there between what it takes to be 'a good teacher' and 'a good manager'?

17. How is technology influencing approaches to management in schools and how do you envisage this process developing further?

[In the industrial model of school, alongside line management and total quality control,] budgets are kept and scrutinised by accountants, press officers try to ensure a positive public image, and performance indicators are put in place to monitor output variables. Above all, there is concern that the product, that is the student, should be delivered effectively and efficiently in accordance with the requirements of the various customers, for example, employers, government, further and higher education. (Jasper Ungoed-Thomas, 'Vision. Values and Virtues', in *Values in Education and Education in Values* edited by M. Halstead and M. Taylor, [London: Falmer, 1996], p. 144.)

When education is regarded as wealth, and economic categories applied to its development, the educational system can be viewed from three perspectives. *Human Capital Formation* is a perspective which looks to the development of technical knowledge and the acquisition of skills as a necessary part of economic growth. Education is seen as the additive effects of individual outcomes, the building up of an infrastructure, a pool of skilled resources for the economic system. The *Production Function* perspective looks to the efficiency of the use of resources within a system, and seeks to establish an optimum cost-benefit ratio in the running of schools. A third perspective can be termed a *Social Agenda*, and deals with the distribution of knowledge in groups in society, with a focus on who benefits from the educational production of skills. The provision of equal opportunities to all members of society, and also, the lessening of divisions that exist between social groups and classes, are among the items on a social agenda. An appreciation of the pervasiveness of economic models in educational provision, policy model and even school organisation is an important perspective on organizational culture. (David Tuohy, *The Inner World of Teaching* [London, Falmer, 1999], pp. 124-5.)

18. In thinking about school as a business or in economic categories, which of these perspectives is operative, at least for some people, in your own context?

Much of the managerial literature aimed at improving educational practice seems to display a universalism that is blind to cultural differences, curriculum specialisms, the climate of particular communities and the role of traditions as foundations for identity and our outlook on the world. A proper concern for raising standards can so easily slip into the temptation of aiming for standardisation. Atomistic objectives and competencies are described without reference to the perspectives and passions of the people involved, whether these are children, adolescents or adults. A false sense of certainty and the dangerous illusion of control are hinted at as desired outcomes of officially sanctioned programmes of curriculum and professional development.

Yet the kind of predictability expected from such programmes would leave no room for a free response or spontaneity on the part of students and their teachers. The ambiguity, complexity, particularity, creativity, unpredictability, open-endedness and essentially personal dimensions of educational practice can soon be lost sight of when too strong an emphasis is laid on 'managing' education. Too great a readiness to map out performance indicators, programmes of study, attainment targets, development plans, and the scaffolding of teaching and management competencies, can lead to specifications that are too elaborate, leave too little to chance, reduce the possibility of appropriate reciprocity and interaction between teachers and learners, and slip too easily into conceiving education as a technique that requires merely one-way transmission.

A few of the fundamental beliefs and doctrines that seem to lie within much managerial practice:

- the world and other people exist for the benefit of organizational survival, exploitation and expansion;
- human beings can control the world and create a better future if they use the right techniques;
- individuals must be subordinate to greater goals decided by their superiors;
- relationships are fundamentally hierarchical and require clear lines of upward accountability and downward responsibility;
- the nature and condition of work should be such as to extract the maximum from the employee;
- everything worth doing can in some way be measured;
- the future can be planned and colonized.

(Stephen Pattison, *The Faith of the Managers* [London: Cassell, 1997], pp. 161-2.)

---

19. Which of these assumptions are problematic from a Christian perspective and why?

20. How should concerns for leadership and success in the 'business' of school be differentiated from and yet also related to Christian concerns about discipleship and salvation?

Managerialism poses three particular challenges for Catholic educators. First, it tempts them to import into schools certain priorities (for example, concern for their market position and success in narrowly prescribed league tables) and certain modes of working (for example, enforced compliance and alignment within the school as an organisation and 'zero tolerance' of failure) that sit uneasily with, even when they do not directly contradict, key features of Catholic education. Second, by pressurising school leaders to establish ever-increasing levels of control over key aspects of teaching and learning, it underlines the dangers of a one-sided emphasis on distinctiveness within the context of Catholic education. Without an adequate emphasis on inclusiveness, new control mechanisms in the service of an authoritative, universal and unavoidable mission can become overbearing and pay too little attention to local realities and needs. Third, managerialism lacks an adequate 'story', one that is well-founded, critically informed and tested over time, a 'story' with the capacity to inspire. It lacks an overarching narrative that connects up school, culture and life, offers a guiding framework and a sense of direction and purpose for education. The 'emptiness' of the arena in which managerialism operates, in that it fails to take into account social, moral, political and religious principles and values, should prompt Catholic educators to re-present their own account of the nature and purpose of education as an important resource for rectifying the shortcomings of managerialism.

There *are* benefits in treating school as a business. If school is part of our life journey and if we should always be open to the transcendent during this journey, this should not blind us to the need to attend to the here and now, nor should it prevent us from ensuring that the vehicle in which we travel and the routes over which we pass are kept in good running order. To be unbusinesslike serves no one well. Such an approach is likely to demonstrate a cavalier attitude towards the quality of what goes on and to fall short in responsible stewardship of the resources, goods and talents for which we are accountable. However, an excess of managerialism subordinates individuals and sacrifices them to corporate goals. It gives a wrong idea of 'worthwhileness', identifying too closely our inherent and eternal value with our current performance and temporary function in some particular (and limited) setting.

RECOMMENDED READING

Bottery, M., *The Ethics of Educational Management* (London: Cassell, 1993).

Bridges, D. and McLaughlin, T. (eds), *Education and the Market Place* (London: Falmer, 1994).

Correia, J., *Business Management in the Catholic School* (Washington, DC: National Catholic Educational Association, 1998).

Grace, G., *School Leadership* (London: Falmer, 1995).

Gunter, H., *Rethinking Education: The Consequences of Jurassic Management* (London: Cassell, 1997).

Jonathan, R., *Illusory Freedoms: Liberalism, Education and the Market* (Oxford: Blackwell, 1997).

Murgatroyd, S. and Morgan, C., *Total Quality Management and the School* (Buckingham: Open University Press, 1993).

Pattison, S., *The Faith of the Managers* (London: Cassell, 1997).

CHAPTER FOUR

SCHOOL AS CHURCH

In all the principal Roman documents on Catholic education it is always made clear that the Catholic school is to be considered as an integral part of the Church's mission. 'The ecclesial dimension is not a mere adjunct, but is a specific attribute, a distinctive characteristic which penetrates and informs every moment of its educational activity, a fundamental part of its very identity and the focus of its mission.'[1] The Catholic school is described as an 'instrument' of the Church, not only a place for education, but also a place of 'evangelisation, of authentic apostolate and of pastoral action.'[2] The Catholic school, whatever it owes to the local community in which it is situated, should always reflect its ecclesial nature. 'It is the Church, after all, which endows the school with its particular edge, its ideological motivation, its social dimension, its global awareness, its moral emphasis, its religious conviction, and the sense of eternal consequences for temporal affairs charges its communal activities with meaning.'[3] The intimate and inescapable connection between Church and school suggested by such notions can be explored from a number of angles. This connection is open to various interpretations, some of which conflict. Several of these interpretations are highly controversial within the Catholic community.

In this chapter I bring into focus some of the implications for school leaders of envisaging Catholic schools as part of the Church's mission and I expose some of the underlying ambiguities that arise from different and developing ideas about the nature and purpose of Church. In section one it is suggested that there are six immediate ways in which conceiving of the school as part of the Church can be expected to modify significantly the work of Catholic school principals. In section two there is a brief sketch of key elements of the ethos that prevailed in the Catholic Church before Vatican II. This should serve two purposes. First, it aims to provide a baseline for clarifying later in the chapter the extent of the changes that have occurred in the Church's self-understanding within a relatively short period of time. Second, it hopes to prompt school leaders to reflect upon the continuing influence on present attitudes and practice of their own past experience and upbringing in the Church. Section three marks out central features of that theology from 'above' that held sway earlier this century and it contrasts these with characteristic aspects of theologies from 'below' that have been influential since the mid 1960s. Section four focuses directly on the shift of emphasis that has taken place in thinking about the Church. Next are highlighted some of the tasks that flow from an acceptance of the belief that a Catholic school is a microcosm of the Church. In this fifth section an indication is also given of some major obstacles that must be negotiated if a healthy Church community life is to be enjoyed in the school context. Finally, three challenges for any school claiming inspiration from the gospel are underlined: evangelisation, ecumenism and the option for the poor. If the general analysis presented in this chapter has any cogency, and if the Catholic principal is to allow full scope for the flourishing of the school as Church, it follows that a confident theological 'literacy' will be a necessary element in any formation and preparation for this role.

1. IMPLICATIONS OF MISSION

If the notion that the Catholic school is an essential part of the Church's mission is accepted, there are immediate implications for the nature, scope and priorities for leaders in such schools. First, one might examine the content of teaching; for example, is specific and authentic teaching provided which does justice to the principal tenets of Catholicism? Do students emerge from Catholic schools sufficiently informed about Catholicism in all its dimensions? Second, there should be a serious attempt to permeate the curriculum with Catholic perspectives and a Catholic 'worldview' so that the interconnectedness that is at the heart of the faith is evident to students and to those who monitor their progress. These first two points are closely interconnected.

Third, the pattern of teaching-learning relationships, the style of pedagogy adopted, and the emotional 'tone' of exchange and communication that is registered in classrooms, should jointly cohere in displaying a concern for the dignity of all, mutual respect, integral human formation and a spirit of love and freedom. Fourth, the 'climate' and the ethos of the school community should be conducive to the flourishing of Gospel values, appreciative of the uniqueness and giftedness of each member and seeking to enhance and to harness these gifts for the common good. It should not be harsh, punitive, unforgiving or impersonal. These two points are also closely linked.

Fifth, within the life of the Catholic school community, one might consider the priority given to and the creative energy and resources devoted to the fostering of personal prayer and public worship, drawing upon the richness of the Catholic liturgical tradition and its diverse forms of spirituality. If this is given a high priority, it will spill over into each of the first four implications already indicated.

A sixth implication of envisaging school as part of Church is for the 'boundary management' role expected of all institutional figureheads. By 'boundary management' I am referring to all those issues that have a bearing on the establishment and maintenance of the particular identity of the school as Catholic. Boundary management will be affected by policies relating to student admissions and staff recruitment. It will also be influenced by decisions about the kinds of behaviour that merit exclusion from the school. Marketing and promotion of the school through various media and in diverse contexts will also have a part to play. Boundary management embraces the defence of an institution's reputation and advocacy of its mission in the external forum. It often requires interaction with sponsors, funding agencies and external agencies with a stake in the school. Relationships with partner schools and with competitors must be worked at. Joint action in support of or in opposition to local and national policies that impinge upon the school sometimes has to be negotiated and co-ordinated.

1. Which of these six areas do you feel most confident about in your own school? Which do you feel most needs further attention?

With regard to the identity of their schools, Catholic principals often have particular 'constituencies' and interests that modify their roles and priorities in ways that distinguish them from leaders of other schools. Being part of a universal Church, belonging to a particular diocese, perhaps working under the trusteeship of a religious order – all these can make an important difference. The imperative to live in accordance with gospel values, the notion of spiritual leadership and the priority given in Catholic teaching to partnership with parents, who are seen as the primary educators of their children – all these should be part of the 'ground-rules' that are in operation.

One of the more obvious ways that Catholic schools in the past have been seen as intimately connected to the Church is the part played in them by men and women who were members of religious orders. These 'religious' staff played a particularly powerful role in embodying the 'Catholic identity' of a school. Their explicit vocation, marked by particular charisms and spiritual traditions, a celibate lifestyle, a lengthy period of personal formation, international connections, distinct clothing and separate community life, clearly contributed significantly to the development of the Catholic school system in many countries and it offered a counter-cultural, even a *contra mundum* stance. However, in the light of changes in Catholic understanding of the Church since Vatican II, it is a little more problematic to assume that the presence of religious can give schools their Catholic identity, even if they were available in sufficient numbers. A major task still faces Catholic schools in building on their legacy and adapting past forms of spiritual formation to current circumstances.

2. CHURCH ETHOS BEFORE VATICAN II

Another way of identifying the Catholic school as part of the Church might be to note the employment (in texts for teachers and in books for Catholic adults in general) of a special language, one deeply influenced by the neo-Thomist theology that was pervasive throughout the Church, especially in the years 1860-1960. From being one style of theology competing for attention alongside several others within Catholicism, neo-Thomism, which is an adaptation of the thought of thirteenth-century philosopher and theologian Thomas Aquinas, was elevated into pole position, made normative for all clerical intellectual formation and fervently advocated as an eternally essential foundation and the sole valid medium for the expression of Catholicism by Pope Leo XIII, for example, in his encyclical *Aeterni Patris* (1879).

Neo-Thomism ensured a certain commonality of theological language between the universal and the local Church; it fostered a particular form of apologetics in the defence of the faith; and it preserved a form of intellectual discipline that was shared by clergy of all ages. It also focused attention on some intellectual concerns, to the neglect of others, being particularly exercised to demonstrate the rationality of faith, the dangers of the Enlightenment and liberal thinking and the incursions of a secular State. In defending an ecclesiology that treated the Church primarily as an institution, neo-Thomist theologians paid insufficient attention to the relevance for faith of personal experience and they also failed to consider the implications of historical understanding.

Although this particular theological emphasis no longer exerts a dominant influence in the Church, it did offer Catholic educators an important and necessary foundation for their work. It provided a rationale for the whole educational endeavour. It gave a sense of direction towards which they could aspire. It articulated a cohesive and tightly interconnected web of thinking about human nature, its predicament as subject to sin and weakness, and the remedy for this parlous state through the authority, disciplines and spiritual gifts offered through the Church. Catholic education (indeed, any form of education that claims to be Christian) always rests upon some kind of theological foundations. 'Christian theology is the architectonic science that furnishes the basic postulates of the theory of Christian education, specifies its objectives, invests the whole process with a distinctive atmosphere, and gives unity and hence intelligibility to its concrete programme. In a word, I assume that Christian theology gives to Christian education what Newman would call its "idea".'[4]

Catholic educators cannot now rely on one consistent, strongly reinforced system of theology in the same way as did their predecessors, nor do they benefit from an extended period of personal formation. They do, however, have available to them rich theological resources that, once assembled, jointly cast light on their context, role, priorities and purposes. Modern Catholic education relies implicitly, if not always explicitly, on developments in the theology of creation and Christian anthropology, and in Christology, ecclesiology and sacraments. There has also been a renaissance of interest in spirituality and a whole host of easily available resources that support the spiritual reflections, prayers and development of lay people.

2. (a) How would you describe your own theological education and spiritual formation? (b) Who or what has been most influential in exciting your interest or dampening your enthusiasm with regard to understanding Christian theology? (c) Which aspect of theology do you feel most interested in? (d) Which part of Catholic teaching strikes you as most powerful and most relevant for the task of Catholic education? (e) If you were asked to give a talk to a group of parents on one aspect of Catholic teaching/theology, in order to demonstrate its relevance either to family or to school life, what would you choose to focus on? (f) What have been the helping and the hindering factors in your own spiritual formation?

3. THEOLOGIES FROM ABOVE AND BELOW

One way to describe the change of emphasis within Catholic thinking is as a shift from a theology from 'above' to one that emerges from 'below'. This shift alters the emotional tone, the ethos or spirit and even the methodology employed in Catholic thinking, about life as a whole and about education in particular. A theology from above may be described as one that begins with, and continues to stress, the transcendence of God, the divinity of Christ, the objective nature of revelation and dogma and the holiness of the Church. It teaches the necessity for obedience to (a divinely established) hierarchical authority, and the importance of historical tradition. There is a clear separation between the teaching Church and the learning Church; teaching is reserved for an elite; the majority has only a passive role in receiving this teaching; communication is mostly one-way, from above to below. Such a theology tends to denigrate the natural, which has to be left behind in order to attain the supernatural; this world is often envisaged in such theology as a vale of tears and as a source of temptation. The priority here is that God has spoken and that we must attend to his word. Such attention to God is to be directed principally via the institutional church and away from self.

A theology from below, on the other hand, offers a different emphasis, without necessarily contradicting the teaching of the theology from above. It stresses the immanence of God, the humanity of Jesus Christ, and the pilgrim nature of the Church. It looks for a subjective readiness for revelation and dogma and an active reception of these. All members of the Church have something to teach as well as something to learn. Communication is multi-lateral and relationships are based on reciprocity and mutuality. Such a theology encourages the full participation of all the people of God in the life of the Church and it adopts a positive attitude towards the world. While tradition is still valued, there is a much greater orientation towards the present and the future, and both the development of doctrine and the living nature of tradition are emphasised. In a theology from below, one is encouraged to seek for God within, to plumb the depths of one's own experience.

Each of these approaches has strengths and each has weaknesses. Whereas a theology from above might, because of its emphasis on the 'vertical', lead to the isolation of Catholics in society, a theology from below can, because of its emphasis on the 'horizontal', lead to their assimilation. The former is strong on defending the distinctiveness of Catholicism, while the latter is more effective in advocating the essential inclusiveness that must be at the heart of Catholicism. If a theology from above stresses our need to accept God's message of salvation, whole and entire, however uncomfortable this may appear to us, a theology from below sometimes seems to allow for an accommodation of human nature and needs to such a degree that God's word is domesticated. The former can appear to diminish us; the latter can seem to diminish God. In a theology from above, a command or dominating model seeks uniformity and suppresses diversity; but a theology from below can seek a false kind of egalitarianism, which fosters diversity at the same time as it fails to facilitate unity.

A theology from above seems to give priority to doctrines while a theology from below appears to give priority to people. Furthermore, while a theology from above stresses the universality of God's offer of salvation and call to holiness – the same message, to all, in the same way – a theology from below gives more recognition to the diversity among all of and within each of us. This opens the way towards a differentiated approach to the communication of religious truth. In one theology, consistency is a major virtue; in the other, flexibility. For the first, preservation of the sacred message (and gifts) is the principal task; for the second, it is creativity in their reception and application.

3. Which aspects of these two approaches, from above and from below, do you recognise as having been influential in your own experiences and observations of the Church?

The problem of religious pluralism is often taken to be about how one brings Christ *to* a culture. This is the heart of the old problematic: the 'other' religious tradition is seen to lack Christ. The new problematic begins *with* culture and, by seeking out the signs of the Spirit, asks how one can speak of Christ being *already there*. ... It is only when I have someone prepared to listen to me that I learn how to speak. And only when I learn how to speak do I know what it is that I have to say. The conversation helps both partners to articulate their experience, to become not 'other' but truly self. (Michael Barnes, *Religions in Conversation* [London: SPCK, 1989], pp. 166, 180.)

4. If one replaced the word 'culture' by 'student' in the above quotation from Barnes, what significance might there be for a teacher in a Catholic school?

Strong communities can be pockets of intolerance and prejudice. Settled stable communities are the enemies of innovation, talent, creativity, diversity and experimentation. (Charles Leadbetter, quoted by Laurie Taylor in *The Guardian*, 21 July 1999.)

5. What implications, if any, might there be if Leadbetter's comment was applied to school as an expression of a (strong) Church community?

4. SHIFT IN EMPHASIS

Some features of the Church's self-understanding before Vatican II have been criticised by Avery Dulles as serious distortions of her true nature. Among these errors he includes triumphalism,

clericalism, juridicism, papalism, dogmatism and ritualism.[5]
Triumphalism displays arrogance about the superiority of the
Catholic Church over all others and proclaims its inevitable
triumph over all adversity and opposition. Clericalism
exaggerates the differences between the ministerial priesthood
and the priesthood of all believers and divides the Church into
first-class citizens – the clergy, and second-class citizens – the
laity. Juridicism exalts the place of law within the Church,
reduces morality to obedience and obscures both the gratuity of
the gospel (which comes to us as a gift and cannot be earned)
and the freedom it offers. In similar fashion, papalism,
dogmatism and ritualism exaggerate respectively the
importance and role of the Pope, of the exact and uniform
expression of doctrine and of precise rules for liturgy, each of
which has a legitimate place in the overall 'economy' of the
Church.

This stance was to be significantly altered both during and
in the aftermath of the Second Vatican Council (1962-5). The
modern world had been rejected and liberalism had been seen
as threatening ecclesial truth-claims by its indifference,
disguised as tolerance. This negative stance was reversed.
Dermot Lane describes the new stance as one that displayed 'the
ecclesial recognition of other churches, respect for the value of
non-Christian religions, the affirmation of the principle of
religious freedom, the acknowledgement of the importance of
human rights and social justice, the endorsement of a "new
humanism", and a real concern for the salvation of the world'.[6]

The Council gave respectability and prominence in Catholic
thinking to notions of collegiality, pluralism and diversity, the
social apostolate, and a more inclusive attitude within the
Church. For instance, it moved away from considering the
Church as being simply co-extensive with the Catholic Church,
or as identical with the Body of Christ, or even more narrowly,

as something to be equated with the hierarchy.[7] Its deliberations prompted a rethinking of key concepts that have a bearing on education: truth, knowledge, salvation, humanity, conversion and revelation. Important Council documents were issued which re-expressed the mind of the Church with regard to its own nature and constitution, to revelation, ecumenism, the role of the laity, missions, non-Christians and religious freedom. Cumulatively, these added up to a significant modification in self-understanding and in the stance to be adopted towards the world.

One major shift in emphasis was to encourage a more positive attitude towards the world and a greater willingness to become involved with others outside the Church in human struggles for justice and peace, as opposed to a stance that had been more withdrawn, isolated and tending to avoid contamination. In tracing the changes brought about by Vatican II, Richard McBrien observes: 'Pre-conciliar Catholicism tended to limit the essential, or constitutive, mission of the church to preaching, teaching, catechesis, and worship (understood as the whole sacramental life). Ecclesial engagement with the wider world through ministries of justice and peace, for example, was regarded as only antecedent or preparatory to the essential mission of the church. A sharp distinction, therefore, was maintained between the sacred and the secular orders'.[8]

In rapid succession, Catholic theologians entered into serious dialogue with a host of thinkers from other intellectual traditions, movements and disciplines, and in the process their understanding and expression of Catholicism was transformed. Debate ensued with existentialists, Marxists and feminist. The categories and perspectives of sociology and psychology were welcomed for the light they cast on the genesis and development of religious ideas and the functioning of religious bodies. New understandings of 'wholeness' and spirituality were gleaned from secular sources and from other religious traditions.

By comparison with the earlier neo-Thomist emphasis, post-Vatican II theology often displays a noticeably different style and tone: it seems less confident and certain; it relies less on logic; it is less imperialist; it adopts a historical rather than a classical mentality; it gives greater weight to co-operation and dialogue with those who are outside the Catholic community and it brings out more clearly the social implications of gospel teaching. This has led to changing expectations of the laity in the life of the Church and also, to some degree, a recognition that the experience, perspectives and contributions of women have been neglected by theologians and Church authorities. Religious education in Catholic schools after the Council reflected some of these changes: its central focus was not so obviously doctrinal; its tone was less dogmatic and authoritarian; it adopted more frequently a multi-dimensional approach to the study of religion; it sought more explicitly to take into account the experience and viewpoints of students; it was more open to criticism and questioning; it was more hospitable to and positive about non-Catholics.

Avery Dulles, one of America's leading Catholic theologians, has provided an extremely influential summary of this changing ecclesiology in *Models of the Church*.[9] Dulles analyses models of the Church as institution, as mystical communion, as herald, as sacrament, and as servant. He brings out very clearly the strengths, weaknesses and attendant implications of each model, and in reviewing them he comments: 'None of these approaches is invalid, none superfluous, and none by itself sufficient' (p. 150). Each of these models has particular insights; but each of them is also open to distortion and imbalance if treated in isolation from the others.

For example, those who adopt the institutional model can fall into the danger of identifying the Church only with its formal structures; they can be doctrinaire, rigid, conformist and, by mistaking the official Church for God, even idolatrous. The herald model may oversimplify the process of salvation, conveying an impression that the *only* task of the Church is the proclamation of the gospel. The mystical communion model may raise expectations about its life that are impossible to satisfy and may, through lack of emphasis on formal structure, lead to confusion when there are disputes to be settled. The sacramental model can be heavily theological, hard to communicate, undervalue structure and attend insufficiently to its mandate for mission. The servant model can run the dangers of reducing the gospel to good works, uncritically accepting secular values and neglecting the spiritual dimension of Church life.

Dulles (p. 181) suggests seven criteria that might be applied in an attempt to evaluate each one of these models: its basis in Scripture, its basis in Christian tradition, its capacity to give Church members a sense of their corporate identity and mission, its tendency to foster the virtues and values generally admired by Christians, its correspondence with the religious experience of people today, its theological fruitfulness, and its fruitfulness in enabling Church members to relate successfully to those outside their own group.

- What image of church nourishes teachers personally and gives them hope?
- How do teachers see themselves participating in the mission of the church?
- What image or understanding of church do they hand down to their students?

- What practices in the church cause concern for teachers, eroding credibility and leading to irrelevance – 'a church out of touch!'
- What practices in the church build credibility?
- Granting that for many the school is where young people experience the church first, what are the implications of the new ecclesial reality for teachers in the Catholic school? (James Mulligan, *Formation for Evangelisation* [Ottawa: Novalis, 1994], p. 59.)

In *The Catholicity of the Church* (p. 10), Dulles refers to four dimensions of Catholicism: (a) its height, Catholicity from above, related to or in communion with the fullness of God in Christ, the divine component; (b) its depth, or its rootedness in the natural and the human; (c) its breadth, or spatial universality; and (d) its length, or temporal extension.

6. Which of these four aspects of Catholicism do you think is reflected most strongly in your school: (a) its acknowledgement of the divine and of Christ as its foundation; (b) its close connection with human development; (c) its welcoming and expansive inclusivity; or (d) its drawing upon a sense of history and tradition? Which of these four aspects is most in need of further attention, emphasis and support in your school?

Bruno Brinkman suggests that 'those who have interiorized Vatican II values find themselves at loggerheads at least intellectually with those who have become restorationists in favour of the status quo ante', and he identifies eight major points of tension: (1) individual leadership versus the doctrine and desire to see the church as the People of God; (2) a general and universal leadership as against the leadership types of local cultures; (3) the issue of salvation within and without the Catholic church; (4) the polarity between the timeless and placeless heaven as a personal inspiration which may vie with the struggle for justice very much in the midst of this world; (5) the old question of biblical supremacy on the one side and the authority of church tradition on the other; (6) the church priesthood being on the one hand a priesthood of all believers in the church, and on the other side the priesthood historically understood, as we know it, of only a selected class, all male; (7) a liturgy which reflects the ancient culture of the West, and the need for liturgies that reflect a variety of cultures; (8) a consecration to God in human lives which have fled the world, over against a form of prophetic witness to be lived within the world where it is most needed.' (Bruno Brinkman, 'Due Veduta di Roma', The Heythrop Journal, vol. 37, no. 2, April 1996, pp. 187-8.)

7. Which of these points of contention are most 'live' or relevant for you and/or the people within your school or associated with it?

8. (a) What changes in emphasis, organisation, style and communication within the Church are needed, in your view, for the healthy continuation of Catholicism into the future?

(b) What must remain the same if Catholics are to be true to God's message and to their tradition?

5. TASKS AND OBSTACLES

If school is to reflect the Church from which it is founded, there will be a twofold movement that must constantly be held in rhythm and balance. A Church school must help its members to look *at* Christ, in order that they are enabled to look out at the world *as* Christ. That is, adults, children and young people must focus on, study, learn about, reflect upon and become familiar with the life and teachings of Christ, and further, develop a deep personal relationship with Christ through Scripture, religious teaching, private prayer and public worship, celebration of the sacraments and charitable works. These experiences should make it possible for them to envisage the world in a Christian perspective, to see the world as Christ does, to be his ears and hands, to respond to people and to creation in a Christlike manner and spirit.

In this twofold movement, some of the time we are inviting members of the school community to be come in and be *with* us; we offer welcome, acceptance, a sense of belonging, recognition and affirmation. At this stage we are shepherds, offering protection, support, formation, upbuilding and a receptive space, with room to be themselves, in a pastorally hospitable environment. This is always with a view to sending them *from* us, where we provide direction and challenge, expecting students to be equipped and ready to serve others and to exercise a prophetic role in the world. In the words of *Gaudium et Spes* (43), we hope to 'cultivate an informed conscience' that leads graduates from our schools to 'impress God's law on the earthly city'. It is an important part of being Church that we use the experience of being part of a 'God-given, Christ-centred, Spirit-empowered community of salvation'[10] to prepare students to carry out their secular vocation, to 'engage in temporal affairs and to order them according to the plan of God'.[11] Far from drawing people away from the world, making them inward-looking, focusing only on Church affairs and on the religious community, we must never lose sight of the fact that all forms of ecclesial 'belonging' and all types of ecclesial nurturing are carried out with a view to 'sending out'. The Christian community is not a holy huddle of the timid or the withdrawn in hiding. It is fed for mission. Any form of retreat is merely a temporary space to allow for a strengthening and equipping for active service.

9. To what extent is your school able to demonstrate that it is preparing students to carry out a secular vocation, to see their work in the world as collaboration with God's grace in building the Kingdom, to be ready to 'contribute to the sanctification of the world, as from within like leaven, by fulfilling their own particular duties'? (quoting *Lumen Gentium*, 31)

If teachers themselves do not have a strong sense of vocation, if they lack the capacity and the confidence to articulate how their own 'secular' work, in all its professional dimensions, can be interpreted as a mode of contributing to building the Kingdom, then it will be much more difficult for students to grow into this awareness. 'The life of the Catholic teacher must be marked by the exercise of a personal vocation in the church, and not simply by the exercise of a profession... It is very desirable that every lay Catholic educator becomes fully aware of the importance, the richness, and the responsibility of this vocation.'[12]

This is not to assume that the influence between teacher and student moves only in one direction. Students exert considerable influence on their teachers, just as children do on their parents. Without such reciprocal and mutual effects, school relationships would not be fully educational; they would lack flexibility and responsiveness and could slip into tyranny and domination. If it can justifiably be claimed that 'most parents are baptised by their children', in that they are simultaneously both 'displaced' and 'consecrated' by them,[13] then it is also true that most teachers are not only taught by their students but even confirmed in their faith conviction and understanding of vocation, in the very course of being tried sorely and tested severely.

However, one must presume that the primary responsibility for cultivating a sense of vocation rests with the teachers, rather than the students. The synthesis between culture and faith that is one of the goals of Catholic education should be evident in the life of the teacher.

As a visible manifestation of the faith they profess and the life witness they are supposed to manifest, it is important that lay Catholics who work in a Catholic school participate actively in the liturgical and sacramental life of the school. Students will share in this life more readily when they have concrete examples: when they see the importance that this life has for believers. ...It is very important that they also have the example of lay adults who take such things seriously, who find in them a source and nourishment for Christian living. (*Lay Catholics in Schools*, 40.)

It might well be objected at this point that the picture being constructed so far in this chapter appears naively benign. It is vulnerable to the accusation that it leaves out of account two major difficulties, which, when taken together, jointly smudge or obscure the picture, and as a result complicate and intensify the problematic task of working in the light of the metaphor 'school as Church'. The first of these difficulties lies in the less than ideal reality of Church life, and the second lies in the less than ideal example of teachers. No doubt these two are in some way connected; inadequacies in the behaviour of teachers in the context of the Catholic school derive, at least in part, from defects in the self-understanding and from shortcomings in the life of the Church. It could be contended that defects in the Church and deficiencies among teachers often converge in the display of a lack of inclusiveness. I will address the issue of inclusiveness as a pedagogical virtue in chapter six. Here I focus more broadly on the Church. Certainly some people see the Church as a 'compromised institution, one with too much blood on its hands, spiritual fat on its body, and too many skeletons in its closet'.[14] As Ronald Rolheiser says , 'all communities of faith mediate the grace of God in a very mixed way. Sin, pettiness, and betrayal are always found alongside grace, sanctity, and fidelity' (p. 120).

When it comes to the realization of the ideal, the most stubborn enemy has always been the sheer nobility of the ideal itself, which – even apart from hindering circumstances – tends to defeat performance. The failures of Christian education are normally multitudinous, sometimes scandalous, and occasionally spectacular. Even at its best a school is only ... one milieu of influence among others. ...What matters in any age is the idea that inspires its efforts, and the integrity of these efforts. (John Courtney Murray, quoted in *Bridging the Sacred and the*

Secular, (ed.) Leon Hooper [Washington, DC: Georgetown University Press, 1994], p. 141.)

The clerical Church is far more visible than the lay Church, and it is easy to make the mistake of thinking that what is more visible is thereby more important. The ordained priesthood is still largely living off the unstated but outdated assumption that the business of the Church is mission and the doers of that business are the clergy. The mission, thus conceived, is to get souls to heaven. This world was a sorrowful and wicked place best left alone.... If instead the task in hand is the evangelisation of this world, then the relationship between the clerical Church and the lay Church alters fundamentally. Not only are the clergy not going to be able to do it on their own, they are not going to be able to do it at all. They are not where the world is: it is not their space. ...The institutional Church of England and Wales is still committed to the concept of 'collaborative ministry'. In the old way of thinking, this means lay people collaborating with the clergy. But isn't the reality more likely to be the clergy collaborating with the laity? The priestly vocation will not start to make sense again until that adjustment in thinking has been successfully made, and translated into new ways of doing the Church's business.... In the movement towards God which evangelisation fundamentally refers to, we cannot leave the whole of creation behind us; we must take it with us. We have to sacralize it, not dump it (but we do not have to churchify it). That means making the world a better place: more peaceful, more prosperous, more just, more

> sustainable, more beautiful. Thus a lawyer has a role in the evangelisation of the world *as a lawyer*, doing what lawyers do. Artists, industrialists and dustmen have roles in the evangelisation of the world doing what artists, industrialists and dustmen do. (Clifford Longley, *The Tablet*, 17 July 1999, p. 978.)

The clericalism that was integral to a theology from above has long been a cause of tension within the Church. It was periodically criticised throughout the Middle Ages, when there was a close alliance between Church and throne, and it became a major bone of contention at the Reformation. Throughout the second half of the twentieth century, with growing democratisation of society, significant advances in educational levels among lay-people and radically less deferential attitudes towards authority at all levels, combined with a massive secularisation of social institutions, clericalism has steadily been losing its hold. It has become more resented and it patently fails to address the spiritual or moral needs of our time. The imbalance within the Church between central authority and local discretion is closely linked to a mentality where clericalism predominates and where there is too great a divide between the Church of the people and its officials. As Leonardo Boff puts it, 'the absolutising of a form of the Church's presence in society led to the oppression of the faithful. Institutional arthritis led to the lack of imagination, of a critical spirit, of creativity…. Without popular Catholicism, official Catholicism does not *live*; without official Catholicism, popular Catholicism is not *legitimated* in its Catholic character'.[15] An excess of clericalism leads to a situation where it could appear to some that it is only through the clergy that Jesus comes into our world and into our lives, and that only they can control, or even influence, the language and the priorities of the Church.

10. How would you describe the current balance between clerical and lay responsibility in Church affairs in your area?

11. Do our Catholic schools teach effectively about the rights and duties in the Church of all its members? What would constitute adequate evidence for this?

In a searing and passionate critique of the contemporary Church the theologian (and parish priest!) Daniel O'Leary writes as follows:

Is the church paying too much attention to itself, its hierarchy, its laws, its exclusions and its suspicion of other denominations, of other religions and even of the world itself that it exists to serve?... Are we too protective of our own interests, too mistrustful of the holiness within the 'outsiders', too dualistic in our understanding of the human and divine unity in all life?... There are many who really worry that the church to which they belong has lost track of the beauty, magnanimity, universality, compassion, openness, trust and courage that marked out so distinctively the life of Jesus. (Daniel O'Leary, *Lost Soul? The Catholic Church Today* [Dublin: Columba Press, 1999], pp. 8, 12, 13, 67.)

On a more positive note, he calls for a change of emphasis:

We are called to convince people of their divine destiny; to fire them up with the goodness of their lives; to excite them with the possibilities of which they are capable; to

---

impress on them the unique responsibility they carry for
the salvation of their community and of the whole
world.... [Speaking of his work with parishioners] Part of
my role [is] to walk with them, listen to them, learn from
them and, wherever possible, share, name and celebrate
with them the deeper realities, the richer revelations
about the love and meaning at the heart of their
sometimes routine, sometimes surprising lives.... [As
alternative images of Church he suggests the following:]
farmer of hearts; prophet of beauty; healer of fear; soul
friend to community; weaver of wholeness; voice of the
silent; sacrament of compassion. (Ibid., pp. 39, 44, 75-7).

12. Which, if any, of O'Leary's alternative images of Church appeals most to you and why? Can you add an alternative image of your own?

Of course there is, and always has been, a need for a balance to
be maintained between conflicting images of the Church and
different elements within it. Both Newman and von Hügel
spoke of three dimensions that had to be held in a creative
tension. Newman referred to the three offices of the Church,
priestly, prophetical and regal, while von Hügel relabelled these
as the institutional, intellectual and the mystical elements of
religion.[16] According to each of these writers, the conflicting
elements constantly jockey for position within the church and
must be held in balance, for otherwise damaging distortions
will occur. For example, 'reasoning tends to rationalism;
devotion to superstition and enthusiasm; and power to
ambition and tyranny'.[17]

Just as each element can, if taken on its own, without
correction from the others, lead to distortion, so too Church

schools, like other organisations, have a 'shadow' side that is likely to be influenced by the respective 'shadow' sides of the models of Church upon which they draw. Within the Catholic context, some cultural analyses have identified a 'shadow' side to various expressions of that faith. For example, Rohr and Martos make a number of criticisms.[18] They accuse many Catholics of neglecting much of their own tradition, of failing to display a concern for the common good, of focusing more on external observance than on inner conviction and conversion, of uncritically accepting the norms and expectations of society. Too often, they say, the Catholic Church is strangled by institutionalism, hierarchy and control; it is over-clerical, male-dominated, leaves little room for creative responses and ministry by lay people, is inadequately scriptural, and its reliance on sacraments can slip into a mechanical ritualism. To the extent that Church schools share in the defects of the wider Church from which they stem, their ethos will be overshadowed by some of these shortcomings.[19]

In recent years the movement towards a more collaborative approach to ministry has been an attempt to respond to some of the above criticisms of the Church. Collaborative ministry builds on some of the insights regained at Vatican II, for example, the priesthood of all believers. It seeks to teach and to exemplify equality, mutuality and reciprocity in relationships within the Church. It might be considered part of the inclusiveness that must always be a constituent feature of Catholicism. Collaborative ministry is an attempt to move away from a two-tier Church, to harness the energies and talents of all, to promote collective responsibility, to allow all members of the Church to teach and to learn, to contribute and to receive from one another. As for hierarchy, in much current thinking about collaborative ministry, this is treated, not as a power over the laity, but as a 'structure for ordering and unifying relationships and gifts, a service to communion. Hierarchy is what holds communion together, rather like the membrane in a leaf'.[20] Instead of the Church being divided – on the one hand, a small elite class of professional clerics and, on the other hand, a majority group of subordinate 'clients' or 'customers', with a clear separation between those who give and those who receive the 'goods' and graces that are the 'currency' of the Church – collaborative ministry seeks to foster a situation in which all are fully fledged members, with complementary rights and duties. The work and needs of all are then, as in any large and complex community, co-ordinated and represented by some 'officers' who should function more like public servants than staff in higher military ranks. Mutual service rather than upward obedience should be the prevailing norm.

Collaborative ministry is still in its infancy. Its implementation is patchy, uneven and, as yet, insecure. Long-established patterns of behaviour in the Church cannot be changed in the space of one generation. What happens to priests in training in seminaries will have a bearing on the degree to which collaborative ministry eventually takes root or survives briefly as a merely temporary phenomenon. However, what happens in school will, I believe, have a much greater influence on whether or not collaborative ministry becomes the usual pattern in relationships between clergy and laity. It is in school that a huge section of the public, at an impressionable age, when they are still open to formation, come into contact with a community that seeks to live by the gospel in all its dealings for several hours a day, for many weeks every year. If students experience the 'officers' of the Church as remote, if they see priests as always male and celibate, if their ministers seem always in control, if the Church's leaders are not open to question or vulnerable to criticism, if these leaders present themselves as always giving and guiding and never needing help or requiring advice, then this cumulative set of impressions will prevent the healthy development of collaborative ministry. Such 'ministry' will seem divorced from key areas of their experience, for example, the messiness and complexity, as well as the drives, excitement and disappointments of sexuality. It will appear unfamiliar with the uncertainties and questioning, the vulnerability and anxieties and the process of trial and error and learning from experience that is so much of most people's lives.

13. How would you place your own school in relation to the promotion of collaborative ministry? What is helping? What is hindering progress?

If collaborative ministry is to be experienced, exemplified and explained in the school setting, those with leadership responsibilities there would do well to reflect, both in their thinking and in their conduct, on the advice given by the Bishops of England and Wales to seminary leaders. 'The model of leadership which is visible in senior staff in the seminary needs to embody the principles of collaboration; openness to ideas, consultation of the whole community in appropriate matters, willingness to listen, commitment to building relationships, inclusion of people with varying gifts and experience within the seminary community.'[21] This kind of community consultation was advocated by St Benedict as a feature of how a wise abbot should act with regard to important matters. The Roman principle *quod omnes tangit, ab omnibus tracteri et approbari debet* – what affects everyone should be considered and approved by all – has long been part of the Canon Law of the Church, although it has been honoured more in the breach than by practice. Newman wrote a controversial essay in the mid nineteenth century, 'On Consulting the Faithful in Matters of Doctrine'. It has been suggested that such consultation should be extended today to focus especially on the victims, the saintly and the prophetic.[22]

To maximise participation among the membership of any community is often a good way to maximise the opportunities for learning by all. Since the promotion of learning is the special province of school, it follows that a school leadership style that encourages and facilitates participation will at the same time enhance the quality of learning. Indeed a school that operated on the basis of a command-and-control type of leadership would be likely to foster resentment, passive resistance and apathy among staff and students. In contrast to this, 'participation fosters the human dignity of workers and their full development as persons'.[23] Without such participation, there can be no authentic co-responsibility in decision-making. It is essential that school leaders establish channels for feedback from staff and students. Members of a school community should feel that their voice is heard and respected, even if it cannot be the last word. This becomes even more important if the school is trying to live as part of the Church. If principals operate as if feedback from those who experience school policies and practices is unnecessary, they will not only undermine the school as a learning community; they will also obscure the fact that it shares in the life of the Church.

> Referring to the ineffective way that the Church operates, a recent study suggests:
> [B]ecause the feedback and co-ordination functions of the system as a whole are so under-developed, [local] initiatives are not reported on and evaluated. [H]ence the local learning-gains fail to become part of the wealth of the whole organization. [O]r, [even] more wastefully, after the fact that they are held to have departed in some way from the One True Path, [they are] therefore criticised or repressed. [If it was] continually learning

about the ways of the world, [the Church] could better teach the world about the ways of God. (Desmond Ryan, *The Catholic Parish* [London: Sheed & Ward, 1996], p. 251. [with slight modifications].)

6. A SCHOOL OF THE GOSPEL

A Catholic school, as part of the mission of the Church, should always allow its policies and plans, its priorities and purposes, to be illuminated, inspired, guided and challenged by the teaching of the gospel. It will itself have a major part to play in the ongoing task of evangelisation. There are seven points to make here on the process of evangelisation in school. First, it should be considered the responsibility of all members of the school community, not just reserved for the teachers. Those in leadership positions should seek ways to engage all members of the school community in hearing and responding to the gospel. It should be a major aim of school management to facilitate the contributions of everybody in this encounter with and communication of the gospel.

Second, we need not only to convey the gospel, but also to be ready to receive it from others. For nobody 'possesses' the gospel in any secure or pure way. Our 'hold' on it is precarious and loosened, both collectively and individually, by sin. Therefore we need and the wider Church needs to be evangelised, to be fed spiritually, on a regular basis, just as we need to replenish our bodies materially with food.

Third, this gospel should not be reserved for the explicitly 'religious' life of the school. As part of the Church, a Catholic school should bring the gospel to bear on all aspects of its existence: the budget, timetable, resourcing, curriculum, pastoral care, and its internal and external relationships.

Fourth, it is difficult to remain true to the Church at the same time as adopting or maintaining a position of power or influence, such as seems required by school leaders. The gospel often seems to be spoken most eloquently by those who sense their own vulnerability and the fragility of life, by those who acknowledge the need for humility and those who are open to criticism. This point needs to be taken to heart by school leaders; it must temper their exercise of authority.

Fifth, the work of evangelisation can be expected to have a transforming effect and a critical dimension for any school or Church that engages in this activity. According to Pope Paul VI's encyclical on this subject, *Evangelisation in the Modern World*, the power of the gospel will 'affect and upset humankind's criteria of judgement, points of interest, determining values, lines of thought, sources of inspiration and models of life' (19).

Sixth, the gospel will not be believed, however accurately it is taught in the classroom, if it is not witnessed to and lived out in the life of the school. Teachers are only listened to if they 'walk their talk'; they must live their words, if these words are to live in or be credible for students.

Seventh, any process of evangelisation will need sensitive, imaginative and prudent adaptation in order to address the diverse contexts, the particular circumstances and the special conditions of the people to whom the gospel is being announced and explained. Kevin Treston brings out the different emphases needed in evangelisation, proclamation, dialogue, inculturation and liberation, if people at different stages of their faith journey are to be addressed. Those already involved need ongoing conversion; the withdrawn need reconciliation; those with no apparent religious faith should be invited to accept the Good News and the oppressed to look for signs of hope.[24] He rightly points out that in schools there will be people at all these stages. Therefore evangelisation in school adopt a multi-levelled approach.

14. Which of these seven aspects of evangelisation is most strongly present in your school? Identify one proposal for action that is intended to give an additional boost to evangelisation.

> As it passes through the chain of generations, each with its own spirit, its own controversial situations, intellectual problems, and spiritual needs, the continuous reflection of the faithful is constantly remoulding and recasting its understanding of the mystery of salvation according to the changing human focus from which the object of faith is illuminated. (Jan Walgrave, quoted by Daniel Finucane, *Sensus Fidelium* [San Francisco: International Scholars Press, 1996], p. 482.)

Two particular ways that a Christian school will be a school of the gospel may be highlighted here: the ecumenical imperative and the preferential option for the poor. The first of these is still a somewhat surprising priority for many Catholics who were brought up on a pre-Vatican II version of their faith. They are now being encouraged to do precisely those things that were frowned upon as recently as in the middle of the twentieth century: to pray with, learn from and co-operate alongside their fellow Christians. Indeed they are told, on the highest authority, that ecumenism is an essential, inescapable and supremely important element within the faith of a Catholic Christian. As for the second priority, the option for the poor, while Catholic schools in many countries have a long and worthy record in this respect, it is only in more recent years that the social implications of the gospel have been emphasised. Only since the late 1970s has a preferential option for the poor been identified as a constitutive dimension of communicating the gospel. Brief consideration is given below to these two priorities.

Ecumenism is not just some sort of 'appendix' which is added to the church's traditional activity. Rather, it is an organic part of her life and work, and consequently must pervade all that she is and does. (Pope John Paul II, *Ut Unum Sint* [London: Catholic Truth Society, 1995], 20.)

Ecumenism has never thrived when the participants ignored their own traditions. The dialectical discernment in which each Christian confession has to engage in order to celebrate what is of the Word and Spirit in their tradition, and to repent of what is not of God, can only be done responsibly with a detailed knowledge of the tradition. (Matthew Lamb, 'Challenges for Catholic Graduate Theological Education', in *Theological Education in the Catholic Tradition*, (ed.) Patrick Carey and Earl Muller, 1998, p. 129.)

Sometimes we teach the 30 years of divisions that developed between 1517 and 1546 in more detail than the vents of dialogue and encounter between Protestants and Catholics that have characterised the pilgrimage of reconciliation between 1966 and the present. [Yet] the ecumenical progress of the last 30 years is as dramatic as the alienations of the same period in the sixteenth century. (J. Gros, in *Catholic Education: A Journal of Inquiry & Practice*, June 1999, p. 396.)

Does my openness to the other compromise my loyalty
to my own tradition? Can we allow that members of
other faiths have as much of a role to play in our growth
as we have in theirs? A real human contact with the other
can help us to know our own tradition better.
...Salvation is not the privilege of belonging to the
group, but the gift of sharing in the divine activity. [Can
we] discover the 'shape of grace' at work in the other? (M.
Barnes [1989], pp. 8, 49, 60.)

15. How can a Catholic school function as an 'ecumenical nursery?'

16. What do you think Protestantism most has to teach Catholicism? And vice versa?

Christ is where the needy are; that is where the Church must be
too. How do we ensure that we hear the voices of the
marginalised and of the minorities in our midst? Do we elicit
and learn from their perceptions of both Church and school?
Are we open to the possibility of being converted by the poor
and by those who are not Catholics? God is there as well as here.
A society that is good for the poor will be good for the rest; but
this does not necessarily work in reverse; what is good for the
rest is not always good for the poor.

It is an experience of incomparable value to have learned
to see the great events of the history of the world from
beneath: from the viewpoint of the useless, the suspect,
the abused, the powerless, the oppressed, the despised –

in a word, from the viewpoint of those who suffer. (Dietrich Bonhoeffer, quoted by Austin Smith in 'Ministry and the Inner City', *New Blackfriars*, vol. 68, no. 810, November 1987, p. 526.)

On the renewed emphasis on the gospel mandate for education for justice, the Jesuit Michael Campbell-Johnson says: 'the needs of the poor take priority over the wants of the rich; the freedom of the weak takes priority over the liberty of the powerful; the participation of the marginalised groups takes priority over the preservation of an order which excludes them.' ('Education for Justice', *The Tablet*, 24 May 1997, pp. 667-8).

17. To what extent would you claim that this is true for your school? What would you point to as relevant evidence for or against such a claim?

A theme that has emerged only implicitly up to this point is the need for a reasonable degree of theological 'literacy' or sophistication as an essential part of the repertoire of Catholic principals. It will not be enough for aspiring school leaders to be able to demonstrate their knowledge in relation to pedagogy, the curriculum, administration, the budget, nor even the qualities and skills they possess in relation to managing and motivating people, resources and information. Very often, successful candidates for the principal's position in a Catholic school have given evidence of all these, together with support from a parish priest that testifies to their practice of the Catholic faith in their private lives. In a rapidly changing Church that is set in an even more rapidly changing society, the kind of ministry that is integral to Catholic school leadership can be carried out without the underpinning of a sound understanding of the relevant theology that illuminates the practice of Catholic education. If they lack this understanding, Catholic principals will find it very difficult to engage, in a spirit of creative fidelity, with the areas of liturgy, social action, ecumenism and inter-faith dialogue. They will be hampered in the task of enabling others to explore any potential links and clashes between the Church's tradition and contemporary arts, sciences, culture and technology. Guided by a sound theological understanding, principals can strive to ensure that their leadership style and their management roles serve to enhance rather than to obscure the church nature of the school community. Such an understanding can also help them to appreciate the intimate connections that should exist between their thinking, their prayer and their actions. In this way discernment, devotion and discipleship will mutually reinforce each other in the task of school leadership.

RECOMMENDED READING

Boff, L., *Church, Charism and Power* (London: SCM, 1985).
Boran, G., *The Pastoral Challenges of a New Age* (Dublin: Veritas, 1999).
Catechism of the Catholic Church (London: Geoffrey Chapman, 1994), pp. 173-216.
Doohan, L., *The Lay-Centered Church* (Minneapolis: Winston Press, 1984).
Dulles, A., *Models of the Church* (Dublin: Gill and Macmillan, 1976).
McBrien, R., *Catholicism* (London: Geoffrey Chapman, 1981), chapters XIX, XX and XXIII.

Nichols, A., *Epiphany: A Theological Introduction to Catholicism* (Collegeville, Minnesota: The Liturgical Press, 1996), ch. 7.

Nichols, T., *That All May Be One: Hierarchy and Participation in the Church* (Collegeville, Minnesota, 1997).

O'Leary, D., *Lost Soul? The Catholic Church Today* (Dublin: Columba Press, 1999).

O'Sullivan, O., *The Silent Schism. Renewal of Catholic Spirit and Structures* (Dublin: Gill & Macmillan, 1997).

NOTES

1. *The Catholic School on the Threshold of the Third Millennium*, Congregation for Catholic Education (Boston: Pauline Books, 1998), 11.

2. *Religious Dimension of Education in a Catholic School*, Congregation for Catholic Education (London: Catholic Truth Society, 1988), 33.

3. Joseph McCann, 'The Crucifix in the classroom', *From Ideal to Action* (ed.) Matthew Feheney (Dublin: Veritas, 1998), p. 29.

4. John Courtney Murray, *Bridging the Sacred and the Secular* (ed.) Leon Hooper (Washington DC: Georgetown University Press, 1994), p. 124.

5. Avery Dulles, *The Catholicity of the Church* (Oxford: Clarendon Press, 1985), p. 159.

6. Dermot Lane (ed.), *Religion and Culture in Dialogue* (Dublin: Columba Press, 1993), p. 16.

7. Richard McBrien, 'Before and after Vatican II', *Priests and People*, August-September 1996, pp. 297-302, at pp. 297-8.

8. Ibid., p. 299.

9. Dublin: Gill and Macmillan, 1974.

10. George Tavard, quoted in 'Building up a Civilization of Love', by Bernard Daly, *Doctrine and Life*, vol. 48, December 1998, p. 584.

11. John Paul II, *Christifideles Laici*, 9.

12. Congregation for Catholic Education, *Lay Catholics in Schools: Witness to Faith* (London: Catholic Truth Society, 1982), 37.

13. Ronald Rolheiser, *Seeking Spirituality* (London: Hodder and Stoughton, 1998), p. 117.

14. Ibid., p. 106. Because of this view, Rolheiser suggests (p. 107) that, with regard to the Church, most people 'are on sabbatical'.

15. Leonardo Boff, Church, *Charism & Power* (London: SCM Press, 1985), pp. 85, 87.

16. Nicholas Lash, *Theology on Dover Beach* (London: Darton, Longman & Todd, 1979), chapter 6; the same author's *Easter in Ordinary* (London: SCM, 1988), chapters 10-12.

17. Newman, quoted by Nicholas Lash (1988), p. 138.

18. R. Rohr and J. Martos, *Why Be Catholic?* (Cincinnati: St Anthony Messenger Press, 1989).

19. John Brennan: The Christian Management of Catholic Schools, Northampton, The Becket Press, 1994, p.80.

20. Bishops' Conference of England and Wales, *The Sign We Give* (Chelmsford: Matthew Jamcs Publishing, 1995), p. 21.

21. Ibid., p. 38.

22. The suggestion is that of Gerard O'Connell; it is quoted by Daniel Finucane, *Sensus Fidelium* (San Francisco: International Scholars Press, 1996), p. 345.

23. Terence Nichols, *That All May be One* (Collegeville, Minnesota: The Liturgical Press, 1997), p. 297.

24. Kevin Treston, 'The School as an Agent in Evangelisation,' *From Ideal to Action* (ed.) Matthew Feheney (Dublin: Veritas, 1998), pp. 58-9.

CHAPTER FIVE

SCHOOL AS POLITICAL COMMUNITY

Minimal roles of any political community are normally thought to include defence, law and order and the establishment of ground rules for the allocation of resources in the interest of the promotion of some conception of the good life. The proper upbringing of the young and their preparation to fulfil some future role in the polity are usually considered as essential to the very survival, let alone the flourishing of any such community. Within schools, many functions mirror those expected of a political community. Just as a nation or a smaller political grouping vigilantly protects the boundaries of its territory and jurisdiction, in order to carry out its daily affairs in security and without interference, so too in school a clear boundary is to be maintained, in this case marking out a space that is at least provisionally removed from the affairs of the world. The 'business' of the world is suspended for a while, to allow a different type of activity to be carried out, namely, the 'business' of schooling. Some form of discipline is established, without which teaching and learning cannot take place. Resources of time, energy, attention and materials are distributed in support of learning. Such learning is directed towards some conception of the good life. Just as products and services cannot be developed or exchanged in society without the support of a healthy political community, so too in schools the 'goods' of learning cannot be secured without the deployment of political skills.

In this chapter I consider how an application to schools of concepts borrowed from the world of politics might cast light on the expectations, opportunities and constraints facing

Catholic school leaders. I begin with a general, non-theoretical understanding of 'politics', followed by a consideration of what might be meant by a 'political' reading or interpretation of education. Second, a sketch is provided of the political context and role of school. Third, I explore the notion that schools reflect, at least partly, some of the features of political communities. Here the internal functioning of the school as a (political) community is the centre of attention. Fourth, I bring into focus several of the changes in society that make new demands upon the political skills of Catholic school leaders, highlighting in particular how the presence of pluralism offers a particularly important new kind of challenge to them. Fifth, there is an exploration of the dual nature of schools, as both institutions and communities, and an indication of the delicate balancing act this dual nature demands of school leaders. Sixth, the work of Catholic schools in the community is related to Catholic social teaching, especially in relation to the promotion of the common good. Seventh, I outline some key areas of school life where political skills are required. Finally, I highlight some key priorities for heads of Catholic schools in their capacity as leaders of political communities.

1. THE 'POLITICAL' AND EDUCATION

Politics is a word that is more often used in a pejorative sense than it is envisaged as something positive and ennobling. Used thus, it refers to a tainted activity, one that must be conducted as a necessary evil. At first sight it might appear that politics has no appropriate place in a context, like that of a Catholic school, where the metaphors, models and associated qualities and ethos of both family and Church have such important application. For many people, politics implies shallow 'sound-bytes', self-seeking manipulation of truth, bargaining by appealing to selfish interests, impugning the record or motives of opponents and seeking to attain or to stay in power at all costs.

In this respect there are similarities with common uses of the words 'academic', 'theological' and 'preaching'. If 'academic' can be taken to suggest a line of argument or an activity that is esoteric, abstract, impractical and disconnected from real life, so 'theological' has similar implications for some people: it is nit-picking, irrelevant, and it preserves the elite role of a special group of interpreters of tradition. In the same way, 'preaching' can be taken to imply a self-righteous, accusatory, narrow-minded, fun-destroying and puritanical attitude. In each case this is a distortion of the true meaning of these words, all of which bear a more positive sense.

Politics is taken here to include legislation, execution and adjudication of policy. That is, it is about drawing up the ground-rules for and identifying the priorities of a particular community, it is about putting policy into practice and it is about critically evaluating progress. We can legitimately claim that politics combines a concern for ideas and ideals, the mobilisation and management of people and a desire to make a practical difference in the affairs of a particular community. Confidence in deploying concepts, adeptness in people management and skills in administration are all called for in a political role. Politics is about power, influence and the promotion of interests, about priorities and decisions and about the effective implementation of these decisions in any society. In the process there will always be contests about the sources of authority, the style in which it is exercised and the objects or goals towards which it is directed.

There is as much scope for these contests in school as in any other community. Questions can be asked thus: Whose mandate to lead? Granted by whom? For what purposes? With what powers? Qualified by which constraints? and: Answerable to whom? Furthermore – in the context of Catholic schooling in a democratic society – how can authority and leadership, in service of a mission shared with the universal Church, be related to the fostering of freedom, to the maximisation of participation, to the drawing out of potential, to the striving for perfection, to the encouragement of a critical and creative appropriation of a tradition and to an intelligent and sensitive adaptation to particular cultures, contexts and settings?

As political leaders, principals should ensure that their leadership is educational: it must permit, invite, encourage and inspire effort, growth, initiative, risk-taking and learning. Such leaders must not only proclaim (through speech and writing) what is needed, but also they must model the way forward through their own actions and facilitate, through all the arrangements of school life, opportunities for others to engage effectively with the school's mission and purposes. Without a constant and untiring effort to involve and empower others, those in authority, no matter how legitimate, will find that decisiveness becomes coercive, communication slips into propaganda, and ideals degenerate into ideological slogans. If the capacity of students and staff to share in leadership is not enhanced by school leaders, growth is stunted, development impeded, self-expression prevented, and advances in authenticity and maturity are rendered difficult. Students cannot learn about justice if they do not experience the school as a just place. Nor will they develop the capacity to contribute effectively to a democratic society in the world beyond school if they do not get the chance to practise the arts of representation, consultation, compromise and weighing of arguments, which are some of the prerequisite skills for participation in a democracy.

Politics here is being taken as relating to the deployment of power and persuasion in the service of principles and purposes. In the school context, as in other political contexts, there is an internal diversity of views about priorities. There are also at least some inequalities in the dialogue about community building, because of differences in maturity, knowledge, experience, expertise and status. Resources are always likely to remain in short supply, at least in terms of the vast expectations laid upon schools. In the case of Catholic schools, these expectations are even higher, since they embrace moral and spiritual dimensions that exceed those that are looked for in secular education. The political role of school leaders also embraces the task of marking, defending and monitoring the boundaries of their schools in relation to the local and wider community. Once again, for Catholic school leaders, this boundary role has additional features, for example, protecting the school from influences that could undermine its Christian ethos.

A political 'reading' of education in general and of school leadership in particular could focus on one or more of several possible areas. It might concentrate on the political dimension within schools themselves. It might attend more to the (actual or potential) political role of schools in society. Or it could be concerned about the degree to which external political pressures have intruded upon life in schools and the influence of these pressures on the exercise of educational leadership.

2. THE POLITICAL CONTEXT AND ROLE OF SCHOOL

Helen Gunter offers a searing critique of the managerial movement that has become dominant in the education systems of many countries. Among her comments on and questions about managerialism are the following:

[a] The industry is about controlling teachers and making them compliant with the external policy context, because a fundamental aim of managerialism is to depoliticise organizational behaviour. ...[b] The rapid adoption of the free-market philosophy as liberation

from bureaucracy elevates self-interest and promotes competition at the expense of democratic values. ...[c] Why is my school/college structured the way it is? How is my school/college changing and what are the implications for myself and my colleagues? How can we inform and be a part of the social and political debate about the types of changes taking place? (Helen Gunter, *Rethinking Education: The Consequences of Jurassic Management* [London: Cassell, 1998], pp. 18, 44, 35.)

1. With regard to [a]: (i) To what extent is there any truth in Gunter's comment on making teachers compliant with an external policy context? (ii) What changes, if any, in the internal organisational behaviour of your school might be attributed to either external political pressures or to the phenomenon of 'managerialism'? (iii) To what extent could you claim that your school is being led by the plans it has made for itself rather than by the changes in its external environment?

2. With regard to [b]: is there any evidence to support Gunter's assertion about the erosion of democratic values in education?

3. As for [c]: imagine some of the answers to these questions that might be given by teaching and support staff in your school, those you see as consistent allies and those who adopt, at least sometimes, a more adversarial role.

In the late 1960s, the provocative and unorthodox cultural critic Ivan Illich, who had had a long schooling in the Catholic Church, offered the following comments on the political role of schools in society.

Schools have the effect of tempering the subversive potential of education in an alienated society because, if education is confined to schools, only those who have been schooled into compliance on a lower grade are admitted to its higher reaches. ...Upon the receipt of a diploma the educational product acquires a market value. School attendance in itself thus guarantees inclusion in the membership of disciplined consumers of the technocracy – just as in past times church attendance guaranteed membership in the community of saints. ...The school is now identified with education as the Church once was with religion. Today's agencies of accreditation are reminiscent of the royal patronage formerly accorded the Church. [Government] support of education now parallels yesterday's royal donations to the Church. The power of the school to rescue the denizen of the slum is as the power of the Church to save the [pagan] from hell. ...The difference between Church and school is mainly that the rites of the school have now become much more rigorous and onerous than were the rites of the Church in the worst days of the Spanish Inquisition. The school has become the established Church of secular times. The modern school had its origins in the impulse towards universal schooling, which began two centuries ago as an attempt to incorporate everyone into the industrial state. In the industrial metropolis the school was the integrating institution. (Ivan Illich, *Celebration of Awareness* [London: Penguin, 1973], pp. 96, 106-8.)

Illich here seems to be making several points. First, schools play an important part in deciding who gets what resources in society. Second, the 'carrots' of potential rewards for compliance and the implied 'sticks' of withdrawal of these rewards – or privileged 'places' in society – exercise a conservative influence throughout the educational process and afterwards. Third, there is a tendency towards totalitarianism within the State-sponsored education system, one that parallels a previously authoritarian Church when that institution had a pre-eminent status in world affairs. Fourth, too much of a person's 'salvation', fulfilment and life chances seem to depend on institutional schooling.

4. What validity is there in any of these four points?

Earlier in the twentieth century, the philosopher Bertrand Russell wrote on the potentially subversive and counter-cultural political role of education.

Instead of obedience and discipline, we ought to aim at preserving independence and impulse. Instead of ruthlessness, education should try to develop justice in thought. Instead of contempt, it ought to instil reverence and the attempt at understanding; towards the opinions of others it ought to produce, not necessarily acquiescence, but only such opposition as is combined with imaginative apprehension and a clear realization of the grounds for opposition. Instead of credulity, the object should be to stimulate constructive doubt, the love of mental adventure, the sense of worlds to conquer by enterprise and boldness in thought. Contentment with the *status quo* and subordination of the individual pupil to political aims, owing to indifference to the things of the mind, are the immediate causes of the evils; but beneath these causes there is one more fundamental, the fact that education is treated as a means of acquiring power over the pupil, not as a means of nourishing his own growth. ...Thought is subversive and revolutionary, destructive and terrible; thought is merciless to privilege, established institutions and comfortable habits; thought is anarchic and lawless, indifferent to authority, careless of the well-tried wisdom of the ages. (An extract from Bertrand Russell, *Principles of Social Reconstruction* (1916) in *Education for Democracy* (ed.) David Rubinstein and Colin Stoneman [London: Penguin, 1970], p. 27.)

5. How strong a feature in your school curriculum is the promotion of independent thinking? What steps might be taken in order to give this greater emphasis?

Very much in keeping with Russell's line of thought, half a century later Anthony Arblaster commented:

Education, rightly understood, is not indoctrination of any kind, but an essentially critical activity. Its function is to encourage people to think independently, to doubt, to question, to investigate, to be sceptical and inquisitive. As such, it is, in any society, a subversive force. ... Education should provide a permanent opposition to orthodoxies, both political and intellectual. Thus education does have a social function, but it is not a subservient one. It is essentially an independent and democratic function. (Anthony Arblaster, 'Education and Ideology', in *Education for Democracy*, p. 54.)

In opposition to the tendency for an unreflective approach to schooling to slip into serving the status quo, there have always been writers who have advocated either a more student-centred or a more counter-cultural form of education; and sometimes one of these in the interests of the other. Thus Jean-Jacques Rousseau in eighteenth-century France, John Dewey in the early years of the twentieth century in the USA, Paulo Freire from the 1960s until the 1980s in Latin America and in various developing countries, and in the 1990s, Padraig Hogan in Ireland.

To take these last two, Freire, in a fusion of Marxist and Christian perspectives, advocated a form of education that moved away from teaching as 'banking', depositing knowledge in an oppressive way into empty vessels, and towards emancipatory pedagogy, something done *with* and not just *to* learners. Education, as the practice of critical consciousness, would make people aware of the conditions – social, cultural, economic and political – that framed their lives, and it would empower them to become agents rather than recipients in the process of education, to function as subjects rather than as objects who are indoctrinated or manipulated by their teachers. Starting with, and deepening their perception of, the problems arising from their own situations, would, according to Freire, lead students to find ways collaboratively to address these problems and to transform their world.[1]

Hogan argues for an invitational form of education that makes learning hospitable to and capable of uncovering each student's unique identity and promise. He builds upon insights from both Freire and Buber in suggesting a dialogic emphasis in teaching, one that appeals to students' attention, efforts and commitments in a form of courtship rather than of imposition or custody. Hogan shows sensitivity to the provisionality of our current state of knowledge and the uncertainties inherent in the processes of education. He seeks to avoid presuming any proprietorial claim on the sensibilities of students. 'Unless the disavowal of such a claim becomes an imperative of professional discipline in teaching, the interplay of influence between teachers and pupils may become rapidly, even irrevocably, disfigured.'[2]

3. SCHOOL AS A POLITICAL COMMUNITY

For schools founded upon the life and teaching of Jesus Christ, any form of education that is true to the radical transformation of self and society, both called for and offered by Christian faith, must display a capacity to 'turn the world upside down'. Thus, part of what Catholic schools must be about is empowerment for change, equipping people for active, constructive and effective involvement in their world. This involvement should also be critical, committed to reducing the gap between reality and guiding ideals. It needs to be courageous and backed up by strength of character, will-power, tenacity and determination to cope with difficulties and setbacks. It must also be wise, capable of discerning the best strategies for winning support and disarming opposition.

School leaders inevitably have a major part to play in fostering this prophetic role of education. They are implicitly authorised for it through the mandate they receive from the Church as a whole, even if this is not fully recognised at the time of appointment, either by themselves or by those who select them for the ministry of Christian educational leadership. Their position in the internal structure of schools means that every action or omission is eloquent with regard to their 'political' stance concerning education. They cannot be neutral as to the role of education in the school, for example, whether it is intended to be liberating or controlling. Every priority, assertion and gesture they display will also carry a message about their views on the role of educated people in the world outside the school, for example, whether they should use their education to achieve a good position and a secure future for themselves or to challenge and to change the world, and in so doing to risk everything by giving themselves away as sacrifices for the sake of a better world. Working at the crossroads of the communication that flows into and out from the school, principals usually have more access to information than anyone else. Their appreciation of its significance and to whom, and their willingness to share this resource, can release energies, elicit hidden potential and promote (among students and staff) the development of the qualities that are essential for commitments that are both wise and loving. Correspondingly, their failure to be politically astute leaves open the door for distorted communication, for baronial in-fighting and micro-political manoeuvring, and for an unproductive waste, perhaps even a destructive use, of energies.

Etzioni identified three ways in which power is exercised, and three responses to that use.

One use of power is *coercive*, whereby people are forced under threat of penalty to behave in a particular way. The typical response to such a use of power is *alienation*, where the participant is negatively or, at best, neutrally involved with the school. The climate developed in such a school is typically coercive, and is characterized by frequent conflict, dissatisfaction and strife.

A second use of power is *remunerative*, where power holders reward participants according to a particular scale for performing their functions. The typical response to such a use of power is that the participants become *calculative* and adapt their involvement to the reward. The climate generated is utilitarian, in that market forces

---

determine the rewards to be offered, and they must be tailored to meet the needs of the individuals involved.

A third use of power is termed *symbolic*, which strives to place a moral imperative to behave in a particular way by appealing to the value inherent in the behaviour. Participants adapt by becoming *committed* to the behaviour and become wholeheartedly and positively involved in the goals of the school. The climate generated is termed normative, in that people are acting out of a conviction of value. (David Tuohy, *The Inner World of Teaching* [London: Falmer Press, 1999], pp. 104-5.)

6. Comment on this analysis in the light of your experience of school 'politics'.

Tuohy (ibid.) continues: One organisational goal is that of *order*, and is typical of organisations such as the army, prison and government. Order goals also exist in schools, in that a large number of people must be co-ordinated and live in some form of harmony. ...Organisations may also have *economic* goals, typical of business and profit-making. ...Schools too can have economic type goals. These typically give rise to a utilitarian climate, where rewards and sanctions are clearly related to performance. However, if an organisation has *cultural* goals, such as those centred on personal values, art and religion, the transactional use of power through coercion or remuneration is unlikely to be effective. What is required here is a climate of shared norms and commitment. Just as there are congruent types between the use of power

> and the response to that use, so also *approaches to power in organisations must be congruent with the goals of the organisation.*

7. What questions arise for you from that last paragraph?

Clearly, any reflection on school as a political community should alert us to the kinds of power being deployed, the manner in which power is used and the ends towards which it is directed. If we wish to be catholic as well as Catholic, then it will be important to ascertain the degree to which the imperative to be inclusive is taken seriously. Sites of power at school cannot help but be influenced, firstly, by the official structure or management model of the school, secondly, by its history and traditions, and thirdly, by the external values, both secular and religious, that are brought to bear upon the school in the form of expectations or even demands.

8. Comment on how these factors influence who and what is authoritative in your school.

9. Traditionally, society has privileged those who are adult, male, white, middle-class and able-bodied. By contrast, women, children, people from ethnic minorities, working-class, aged and disabled people benefit much less from having access to positions of power or decision-making and therefore they have to struggle harder to find a voice and to receive a hearing. How does this relate to sites of power and disempowerment of students and staff in your school?

10. What sorts of modelling of positions of power are offered within your school? What is taught/learnt about power: how you get it? what it's there for? how you use it? In

answering these questions, consider the perspectives of the following: (a) a cleaner at the school; (b) one of the youngest students; (c) one of the oldest students; (d) the youngest teacher; (e) the teacher who has been there the longest; (f) a governor; (g) a parent; (h) the vice-principal.

11. Are there any other relevant factors operating that have a bearing on your understanding of the sources, use and reception of authority, influence and power?

If society is self-governing, then its members must be able to take part in its collective self-management. This means more than simply acquiring rational autonomy, the ability to make up one's mind and exercise independent choice. It involves an appreciation of how others may differ in viewpoint, a tolerance of difference and a willingness to work together despite these differences. It requires an accommodation to the demands of collective decision-making, a willingness to accept those decisions with which one disagrees, and preparedness to play one's part in the execution of decisions. It requires an understanding of what is involved in making a democracy work, a commitment to defend its maintenance, to participate as fully as feasible and to assume the burdens that democratic administration imposes. A citizen must be educated both to and in democracy. [There must be] an inculcation of the civic virtues – tolerance, respect for others' rights and non-violence, among others. At the same time children must learn democratic participation through practice. Active democratic citizens are not born overnight when a certain age is reached. (David Archard, *Children: Rights and Childhood* [London: Routledge, 1993], p. 164.)

12. (a) What rights do students have in relation to their teachers? (b) What other rights do students have in the school context? (c) What rights do teachers have in relation to students? (d) How best can personal and social education in the curriculum, extra-curricular activities, the use of school councils and opportunities for community service help prepare students to understand, appreciate and be ready to participate in a liberal, democratic, pluralist society? (e) What issues are likely to arise for (and be of interest to) students when we use terms like equality, justice, autonomy, privacy, rationality, the exercise of choice, and involvement in decision-making in the school context? (f) Is there any evidence of paternalism in your school? (g) What kinds of 'civic' responsibility can we promote among students in the context of school life?

4. Pluralism and Other Challenges

Different kinds of changes in their surrounding social and cultural contexts present schools with new leadership challenges. Among them the following ten developments can be picked out as particularly significant for schools. (1) Although there are exceptions to the general trend, Catholic schools have moved from being small-scale to being larger-scale communities. (2) Within them there has been a shift from religious to lay leadership. (3) Ever since Vatican II, although with pockets of resistance both in Rome and in local areas, the Catholic Church has gradually been shifting away from a hierarchical and paternalistic style of self-presentation, giving much more emphasis to the central role and high calling of the laity. (4) Public exposure of numerous serious scandals, which provide persistent and painful evidence of past and continuing abuses by members of religious orders or by parish clergy, has led to a crisis of confidence in the institutional Church in many areas and it has weakened the Church's moral authority in society. These changes, taken either separately or together, cannot help but affect the special ethos of Catholic schools.

Many contextual developments, of course, influence all schools, regardless of their religious affiliation or lack of it. For example, (5) where oversight by a Board of Management/Governors was once relatively *laissez-faire*, now evaluation has a high profile and there are greater demands for accountability. (6) The enjoyment of a high degree of autonomy, by schools as institutions and by the teachers within them, has been recently curtailed by increasingly prescriptive government legislation. (7) Having been granted for many years a relatively uncontentious space for curriculum development and experiment, schools are now exposed to public scrutiny and debate, not only about what should be taught, but even how and for how long. (8) In society as a whole there has been a move away from a general acceptance of and respect for the authority of professionals and providers. A decline in deference has been accompanied by a greater sense of the importance of customer orientation and the rights of citizens to call professionals to account. (9) Increasing recourse is often had to litigation over abuses formerly unrecognised or not perceived as seriously unacceptable from public servants. (10) Where once schools were mostly protected from questions about value for money and financial management, now such questions are being posed forcefully and inexorably. Cumulatively, these developments add up to a formidable array of demands upon school leaders.

13. Which two of these changes do you feel have been most significant for your school and how? What difference, if any, do such contextual changes make for Catholic school leaders, either in terms of demands upon them, or opportunities for them (or both!)?

One of the major changes in the external environment, a cultural development that poses new challenges for school leaders, is the emergence of pluralism. First, the degree of differentiation of life-stances among the population has in fact increased, partly due to immigration, partly due to the loss of control of the established Churches. Secondly, and in the wake of this, there has grown up an expectation, on the part of a significant proportion of the population, that such pluralism should be accepted, tolerated and defended, perhaps even welcomed as a desirable feature of a mature democracy.

Furthermore, some would use the increasing pluralism of beliefs and ways of life in society as the foundation for a new purpose for Catholic schools. This would be the deliberate preparation of young people to take their place in such a pluralistic world. Such preparation must equip students with a knowledge, understanding and appreciation of people who are different from them. This needs to be accompanied by the kinds of attitudes and skills that facilitate inter-faith dialogue and multicultural collaboration. Education for pluralist society in all schools, including Catholic schools, should drive out mutual fear, misunderstanding, suspicion, hostility and isolation. In preparing students to face pluralism, it will be important for school leaders to challenge and to support their teachers in the task of creating in classrooms the kind of 'hospitable spaces' that allow young people to experiment, to question, to criticise, to rehearse dissent, to engage creatively with orthodoxy, and to test the boundaries of authority, without at the same time causing undue anxiety amongst parents or a sense of betrayal by local clergy.

I am suggesting that Catholic school leaders should somehow add to the range of their (already too numerous) duties, the highly complex and demanding task of simultaneously protecting and monitoring the advance of pluralism. This role calls for sophisticated political skills. For some principals, the task will be both unexpected and unwelcome. It is something for which they feel poorly prepared and perilously ill-equipped. In fact, schools are at the cutting edge of the Church's developing appreciation of what is entailed by living in a plural world and what is meant by adopting a fully catholic – or inclusive – approach to people. There has, as yet, been little published in the way of practical guidance from the Church to assist school leaders.

An exception to the general paucity of advice is *Catholic Schools and Other Faiths*, a guidance document issued by the Catholic Bishops' Conference of England and Wales in 1996. This demonstrates a very positive interpretation of and response to religious pluralism within society in general and within Catholic schools in particular. However, its implementation by teachers and governors probably requires an increase in the level of theological 'literacy' and pastoral sensitivity displayed by many teachers and governors in Catholic schools.

14. How has the growth of pluralism, in society and in the Church, been experienced in your school? What have been the effects on the task of school leadership?

5. School as Institution and Community

School is an intermediate association. That is, it operates in between the intense familiarity of the home and the potential anonymity of the State, between intimacy and neutrality, between a natural and fervent partiality for particular persons and a constructed and detached impartiality towards all. Its sphere of influence is neither that of the private and domestic nor that of the public and worldly. In between there is the semi-public world of school. Here our inner world is not, for the most part, the main object of our attention. Here we are progressively guided to come to terms with the world beyond us. In the process of engaging with what is strange and 'other' to us, we deepen our understanding of the personal. As we grow in self-knowledge and self-esteem, we find it more and more possible to recognise and appreciate the nature, the integrity, the needs and the 'call' of other people, creatures, practices, institutions and ways of life that are 'foreign' to us. In order to facilitate the appropriate ethos in school, one that builds upon but then gradually moves away from the domestic and familial world, in the interests of continually opening up students to the larger, external world beyond the school, principals must strive to maintain a delicate balance between nurture, support and continuity on the one hand, and disruption, challenge and change on the other.

As leader of an institution and a community, the principal is involved in a dual activity. The organisational or institutional dimension of the role should operate in service of a mission and a community. This is the order of priority: the institution does not 'happen' to have a mission, as if this were an additional feature of its existence, to be considered after the organisational has been 'sorted out'; the mission comes first, a community grows up around it and in response to it, and this community requires an institution to harbour its members, to co-ordinate their efforts and to offer a hospitable 'space' in which its mission can flourish. In another context that mission might elicit a different form of community, and this in turn might necessitate different forms of institutional arrangements.

15. Can you recall, from your previous experience in schools, occasions when the mission of Catholic education seemed to be treated as subordinate (whether intentionally so or not) to organisational concerns and institutional imperatives?

As institutions, schools depend on order, success and reputation. Without these, they fail to enjoy public confidence, their students' chances of employment are reduced and their very economic viability becomes extremely vulnerable. A concern for rules, for efficiency and for measurable 'outcomes' or progress – these are all necessary for the maintenance of institutions. But if institutional requirements dominate the community, rather than serve it, then the mission is likely to be obscured, the legal will be mistaken for the moral, hierarchy will be assumed too readily to be the sole source of authority, and acquiescence and passivity will be settled for instead of conviction and consensus. A telling question here is: how are dissenters among the students and staff dealt with? If trust and credibility are considered to be key ingredients in a school community, then channels of communication must be kept open, non-coercive argument must be fostered, and questioning that is not closed down too quickly or even directed in too disciplined a manner must be encouraged. This requires a high degree of self-confidence and inner security on the part of leaders.

Selznick picks out five elements of community: settings in which people grow and flourish. These are (1) history, (2) identity, (3) mutuality, (4) participation, and (5) integration. By the first he means a sense of sharing a heritage of significant events, both positive and critical, a sense that provides roots. We know where we are coming *from*. By the second, he is referring to feelings of loyalty that derive from effective socialisation and the subsequent identification of self with others; I know who I am, because I know who I am *with*. By mutuality, Selznick intends experiences of interdependence and reciprocity. If people and groups do not need each other, if nothing is to be gained from co-operation, community is not likely to emerge or endure. However, a vibrant community cannot be built on the basis of contracts that specify equal obligations in return for equal benefits. The realities of association may require *unequal* contributions rather than a carefully balanced reciprocity. We need each other and we need different things from each other. The fourth element of a flourishing community is high levels of participation. Everybody matters; each person has a part to play; we can all make a difference. Selznick's fifth element, integration, refers to the degree to which coherence in the norms, beliefs and practices of a community is evident. The various policies and practices fit together and reinforce each other. (Adapted from Philip Selznick, *The Moral Commonwealth* [Berkeley: University of California Press], 1992, pp. 360-4).

16. Which of these five elements of community are strongest in your school and which needs boosting?

6. IN THE COMMUNITY AND FOR THE COMMON GOOD

In Catholic social thought, the community is given a strong emphasis, without slipping into collectivism. Within the community, great importance is attached to the development of persons, without advocating individualism. The Second Vatican Council, especially the Pastoral Constitution on the Church in the Modern World, *Gaudium et Spes (GS)*, underlined the importance of human rights and upholding the dignity of all, as well as respect for subsidiarity and freedom. It offered strong support for democracy and for limited constitutional government and it hoped that opportunities for active participation within the political community would be maximised. These priorities are qualified by a parallel concern for truth, justice and love. While ready to accept a separation of Church and State, Catholic social thought was far from accepting any privatisation of values and beliefs. A perfectionist understanding of politics still underpins Catholic social thinking, despite concerns about the dangers of State intrusion into the realm of family life. According to such a view, government should establish the social conditions conducive to human perfection, foster 'the integral development of the human person', act as guardian of public morality and bring home to the laity their duty to 'impress the divine law on the earthly city' (*GS* 43).

Central to Catholic social teaching is a particular interpretation of the common good. This is a term that can be better understood in the light of two other terms: solidarity and subsidiarity. I shall comment briefly on each of these three. A Catholic school leader, if s/he is to be true to the living tradition of the Church, needs a degree of familiarity with these terms and demonstrable confidence in deploying them in the context of prioritising and then of mobilising people to address these priorities.

The notion of the common good, as taught within the Catholic tradition, has a lengthy history. It draws upon both classical (especially Aristotelian) and scriptural roots. In sacred Scripture, there is a developing theology of creation, of history, of stewardship and of covenant, all of which have a bearing on the common good, the sense of a communal relationship with God, and, through God, with each other. The legal and liturgical elements in Scripture also reinforce the strong emphasis on community and the common good. I take the broad meaning of the phrase the 'common good' to refer to 'the sum total of those conditions of social living, whereby men are enabled more fully and more readily to achieve their own perfection' (*Gaudium et Spes*, 26).

In *The Catechism of the Catholic Church*, three essential elements of the common good are identified: 1) 'respect for the person' [so that s/he has room to exercise natural freedoms such as:]...'conscience, privacy, and religious freedom'; 2) 'social well being and development of the group' [which includes a mixture of all that is needed for a human life, such as:] 'food, clothing, health, work, education and culture, information' [etc.]; 3) 'peace and security'. [Although] 'the human good is always oriented towards the progress of the person' [there is an] 'obligation on all to participate in promoting the good'; ...'both personal responsibility and public life' [are essential]... 'Everyone should be concerned to create and support institutions that improve the conditions of life.' (London: Geoffrey Chapman, 1994), pp. 418-21.)

An understanding of the common good is not one that the Church arrives at ready-made, complete and applicable thereafter to all times and situations. What is assumed to be the common good will be dependent on an understanding of many things: human nature, the possibilities and constraints afforded by the level of our scientific 'reading' of and technological capacity to 'manage' the world around us, the possible elements required for individual and social flourishing, the available values that can be realised and the potential threats against which we should guard ourselves. For example, earlier twentieth-century Catholic defences of the common good were directed against totalitarian belief systems such as communism and fascism, which completely subordinated the individual to the needs of the collective.

A recent authoritative, if brief, statement of the Catholic Church's position on the common good is that issued in the autumn of 1996 by the Bishops of England and Wales, *The Common Good and the Catholic Church's Social Teaching* (CGCCST). In this document the common good is defined as 'the whole network of social conditions which enable human individuals and groups to flourish and live a fully human life, otherwise described as "integral human development" '.[3] Underpinning the understanding of the common good that pervades this document, there are two particular ideas that are given prominence: these are subsidiarity and solidarity. 'If subsidiarity is the principle behind the organisation of societies from a vertical perspective, solidarity is the equivalent horizontal principle.'[4] Central to subsidiarity is the desire to disperse authority and to foster the healthy development of a range of institutions and communities that serve as intermediary bodies between the State and individuals.[5] The classic definition and assertion of subsidiarity upon which the bishops draw is that of Pope Pius XI:

Just as it is gravely wrong to take from individuals what they can accomplish by their own initiative and industry and give it to the community, so also it is an injustice and at the same time a grave evil and disturbance of right order to assign to a greater or higher association what lesser and subordinate organizations can do.[6]

Solidarity, on the other hand, is meant to indicate the virtue of acting in the light of our mutual responsibility for one another. It underlines our interdependence. Far from reducing morality to a private, simple or sentimental response, it engages with the complexity of the systems in which we are all enmeshed, economic, cultural, political and religious.[7] Solidarity goes beyond charitable sharing and engages in a radical restructuring of society. Subsidiarity and solidarity are seen to be intimately related, each serving the common good, although in different ways. Subsidiarity should serve to protect and to promote the particular and the local interests of intermediary bodies, while solidarity should ensure that such interests do not lead to excessive narrowness of concern, fragmentation, division, lack of cohesion or a denial of those features of our existence that we hold in common.

There will be some tension between these two, for if a concern to protect subsidiarity is carried too far by any group, this will undermine the concerted decision-making and action by representatives of the whole community. In such circumstances the group might adopt a counter-cultural mode of relating to the wider society. This has sometimes been the stance adopted in secular societies by the Catholic Church. If little room is left for the operation of subsidiarity, because of a too dominant pressure to institutionalise and promote solidarity through collective action, there is a danger that local communities and groups will be stifled, over-dependent on the State, prevented from exercising initiative and forced to confine the practice of their traditions to the private and domestic domain, which would emasculate entirely their claims to offer something of public significance, even to those who are not adherents.

Subsidiarity and solidarity are closely associated, in the minds of the bishops, with other basic principles or emphases: the importance of listening to ideas from others, natural law, the 'option for the poor' and the importance of recognising our social responsibilities.[8] This last is given a broad interpretation:

> Christ taught us that our neighbourhood is universal: so loving our neighbour has global dimensions. It demands fair international trading policies, decent treatment of refugees, support for the UN and control of the arms trade. Solidarity with our neighbour is also about the

promotion of equality of rights and equality of opportunities.[9]

The Bishops stress that democracy depends on common values and an understanding of the common good. They deplore the ceaseless amplification of claims to rights in the name of an autonomy that operates without limits and in a vacuum. Instead, they emphasise that human rights derive from the nature of the human person made in the image of God.[10] They go on to apply these principles to the market place, social services, the mass media, the world of work, Europe, the global common good, the environment, ownership and property, with a recognition of the multiplicity of roles we play:

[a] manager in one enterprise may be the consumer in another, the neighbour of a third, the supplier of a fourth, a shareholder in a fifth; and may subsequently become a redundant ex-employee, the victim of the very policies that as a manager he or she may have helped to create.[11]

[One image of the common good is that of] a corridor in a hotel. Innumerable chambers open out of it. In one you may find a man writing an atheistic volume; in the next someone on his knees praying for faith and strength; in the third a chemist investigating a body's properties. In a fourth a system of idealistic metaphysics is being excogitated; in a fifth the impossibility of metaphysics is being shown. But they all own the corridor, and all must pass through it if they want a practicable way of getting into or out of their respective rooms. (William James, quoted by George Marsden, *The Outrageous Idea of Christian Scholarship* [New York: Oxford University Press, 1997], p. 46.)

17. In what kinds of areas does your school have to show a concern for 'the corridor,' if it is to claim with justification that it both cares about and contributes to the common good of the larger society of which it is a part?
18. Identify those situations or issues where there seems to be a clash between serving the good of other schools and promoting the particular interests of your own school.

7. THE POLITICAL DIMENSION OF SCHOOL LEADERSHIP

In the process of school leadership, many political skills will be called for, if the energies of people are to be harnessed, if resources are to be secured, and if these energies and resources are to be co-ordinated in the service of over-arching values and goals. Principals have to possess both a global view and a local view. This requires developing what is sometimes called a 'helicopter mind', one capable of taking a detached view and seeing the school through the perspective of different outsiders and yet simultaneously rooted in and possessing a detailed knowledge about the functioning of their own school. They need to develop an overview of society and the workings of the educational system so that a realistic assessment can be made about how their own school is situated in the scheme of things, for example, in relation to its share of resources, its relative attractiveness in market terms, and the quality of the education it provides. This global view also entails being aware of how their school is perceived by relevant 'stakeholders', the bearing of national and local policy on the school, and scanning the external environment for both the threats that are posed and the opportunities that are offered to the school.

At the same time they need to retain sufficient of an 'internal' view of how these external developments are perceived within the school to enable them to mediate between the micro-politics of the school and the macro-politics of the education system and the wider society. Such mediation will sometimes require careful sifting of information, relating it to the 'story' from within and repackaging it with a new 'gloss.' At other times it will necessitate cushioning the school from external initiatives that appear to be arriving too rapidly for the school to assimilate or that appear alien to the desired ethos of the school, intrusively upsetting its carefully established priorities and putting in jeopardy harmonious relationships. On some occasions school leaders need to break down the school's relative isolation from the general run of educational developments, tackle an unwarranted complacency, insist on a more positive engagement with the external agenda, in order to ensure both that the school really does provide the best possible service for its students and that the school is not left so far behind current developments that its reputation and survival are undermined. Here the notion of 'constructive confrontation' has application, the willingness and the capacity to address resolutely issues that may be uncomfortable for self and others, but to do so in a manner that leaves intact the dignity of all involved. Constructive confrontation ensures that the appropriate balance is established between, on the one hand, determination and prescriptiveness, and, on the other, conciliation and the offering of positive options. In this way, those confronted still feel able to exercise their own judgement and to own the outcome of decisions, instead of having these simply imposed on them as a crushing command.

Among the other qualities that enhance the 'political' management of school, one might mention the desirability of being receptive to the internal emotional climate in schools and yet also capable of ignoring or even overriding it when necessary. Principals must be prudent in identifying what mechanisms and approaches will offer 'leverage' in moving things forward, without slipping into manipulation, a mode of working that makes people feel that they are being treated as objects rather than as subjects in their own right. They must demonstrate the ability to inspire, to elicit enthusiasm and commitment, yet also they must know when to constrain, even forbid further initiatives at particular moments.

They must maintain a certain distance from colleagues and students, in the interests of both mutual respect and the 'space-making' that allows tentative experiment and provisional judgement. Such distance also functions as a protection against accusations either of favouritism or of having permanently taken a firm dislike of a colleague. Nobody should feel that they have the principal 'in their pocket', nor should anyone feel that their 'face does not fit' and therefore that they have no chance of ever receiving a proper hearing. Furthermore, the experience of disappointment, feeling let down or even a sense of betrayal, can be softened or minimised, to some degree at least, if the principal has maintained a professional distance from colleagues. This is especially important when it comes to difficult and unpopular decisions. These might include, for example, refusing a request that is important to a particular person but that might be unhelpful for the community as a whole, or disciplining a colleague for unprofessional behaviour, or making people redundant, or refusing a pay rise, or discontinuing a project.

If such distancing is carried too far, however, there can creep in an emotional coldness and lack of affection, an impersonal style that erodes the conditions of commitment. This in turn makes difficult another vital political skill, the building of coalitions made up of people with different interests, priorities, and perceptions. Coalitions require a willingness to blur distinctions, to sacrifice something important in the interest of a larger project, and demonstrating sufficient flexibility to elicit co-operation from as many people as possible. Here too, much distance separating leaders and staff does not help in the give-and-take of debate and bargaining.

Discretion, prudence, a keen sense of the signs of the times – these become precious political virtues. Pacing, timing, the ability to marry boldness to restraint all pitch in. To be effective, politicians have to be enough in touch with their constituency to know that the folks back home will support what they have in view. On the other hand, effective leaders do not rest content with what the lowest common denominator makes certain will be popular. (Denise Lardner Carmody, *Organizing a Christian Mind* [Valley Forge, Pennsylvania: Trinity Press International, 1996], p. 117.)

Bringing about successful change requires a kind of leadership which combines qualities that seemingly do not go together: having a clear vision *and* being open-minded, taking initiatives *and* enabling others, providing support *and* pressure, starting small *and* thinking big, expecting results *and* being patient, having a plan *and* being flexible, using top-down *and* bottom-up approaches, experiencing uncertainty *and* satisfaction. (Padraig Hogan, *The Custody and Courtship of Experience,* p. 249, summarising the work of Michael Fullan on educational change.)

Organisations need 'benevolent politicians' who steer a course between naivete and cynicism. ...What political skills does a manager need? ...To develop a sense of direction, build a base of support, and learn how to manage relations with both allies and opponents. This requires at least four key political skills: agenda setting; mapping the political terrain; networking and forming coalitions; and bargaining and negotiating. ...[Attention must be paid to] a *vision* balancing the long-term interests of parties involved and a *strategy for achieving the vision*, recognising the full range of competing internal and external forces. A vision without a strategy remains an illusion. (Lee Bolman and Terrence Deal, *Reframing Organizations*, 2nd edition [San Francisco: Jossey-Bass Publishers, 1997], pp. 178–80.)

Other considerations for leaders faced with conflicting agendas competing for their attention might include those of acceptability, suitability, feasibility and equity. Acceptability relates to the main concerns, expectations and demands of key stakeholders. Suitability seeks a fit or a compatibility between a new proposal and the prevailing (or the desired) ethos and mission of the school. Feasibility explores the implications of a suggestion in terms of the kind of resources of time, finance, training, expertise, support, accommodation or permission it may require. Equity gives consideration to needs, rights, use, distribution of resources, barriers to access; it asks: who wins and loses from particular policies and proposals and how just are they?

The philosophical bases of [political and business] organisations may well be inconsistent with the rationale for the existence and conduct of Catholic schools as expressed in its theology: 'the Catholic school aims at forming in the Christian those particular virtues which will enable him [sic] to live a new life in Christ and help

> him play faithfully his part in building up the kingdom
> of God' (*The Catholic School*, 1977, 36). ...The second
> reason why conventional models of leadership may be
> inappropriate to Catholic schools is that they rely on the
> power and authority of office-holders to achieve
> corporate goals. ...Since Vatican II a more participative
> People of God model has prevailed. (Denis McLaughlin,
> *Leading a Catholic School* (ed.) John McMahon, Helga
> Neidhart & Judith Chapman [Richmond, Victoria,
> Australia: Spectrum Publications, 1997], pp. 11-12.)

**19. How would *you* describe the difference between the
nature and purpose of politics and that of Catholic
education?**

**20. Which qualities, skills or strengths often shown by
political leaders are, in your view, *not* appropriate in the
exercise of leadership in Catholic schools?**

**21. Which of the skills or qualities suggested as part of the
necessary political 'repertoire' of school leaders throughout
this section do you feel is most evident in the way you work
and which ones need further support or fresh efforts?**

**22. Relate this assessment of your own political skills to that
shown by others in your past experiences of one or more of
the following: (a) the successful management of a change in
school that comes from an external agenda; (b) the
unsuccessful management of a change that sought to
respond to external pressure; (c) encountering and
responding to internal resistance to a change initiated from
within the school; (d) coping with external resistance to a
school initiative; (e) co-operative activity between schools to
address a (jointly perceived) external threat.**

> Leadership in Catholic schools should be communal, transformative and serving. It is communal because the power of leadership ultimately resides in and is given to the leader, from the community. It is transformational since the organisational community is ever prepared to critique its action against the original authentic vision which vivifies the community. It is serving because the growth of community members and indeed society is the object of the leadership. It is only when the community is able to share in the leadership of the school that the community can start to grow in the image of Christ. (Denis McLaughlin, op. cit., p. 25.)

23. Give one practical example in each case of what might be meant by (a) communal, (b) transformative, and (c) serving leadership in a school.

24. In what sense is the final sentence quoted from McLaughlin true and in what sense is it, at least partly, a distortion of what is meant by growing in the image of Christ?

There are many areas of school life where the various skills and qualities associated with the political dimension of school management will be needed. I indicate here just some that have not yet received an explicit mention in this chapter. First, there is the task of dealing with the legacy a leader inherits on appointment to a school. Whether new principals are promoted from within or are externally appointed, the way they situate themselves in relation to the style and priorities of their predecessors will be hugely significant in 'political' terms. Here a particular tone is set and loyalties either won or lost, according to the sensitive balance struck by the new principal. What kind of balance is being referred to here? It is a balance between, on the one hand, a demonstrable respect for tradition and the achievements and reasoning that has prevailed up to now (in which many members of staff will have invested energy, commitment and much of their hopes for professional advancement), and, on the other hand, a willingness by principals to 'set out their stall' in their own way, with independence of thought, fresh ideas and a determination to carry them through, having demonstrated that they are well-founded and in the long-term interests of the school as a whole.

Another key area for the application of political wisdom is the way that the Board of Management (the governing body) is treated by the principal. This body will include representatives of the local (business and political) community, of parents and the Church; it may also include representatives of the teaching staff. Relationships with this group can be conflictual, collegial or, in some cases, avoiding conflict at all costs (thereby privileging conviviality over any other priorities). Yet, if the governing body is to be helped to move away from being merely a 'supporters' club' for the school to being a representative group of citizens with a public mandate to shape and monitor school policy, there will be considerable scope for the exercise of political judgement by school leaders. If the governors are to provide a strategic view, to act as critical friends of the school and to ensure accountability, and in the case of Catholic schools, to function as guardians of the mission, then all the skills highlighted earlier in this chapter will be called upon, including persuasive advocacy, agenda setting, the management of information (openness without overload), coalition building, maintaining an appropriate distance and balancing a concern for efficiency with a sensitivity to the personal hopes and fears of the people who comprise the team.

In parallel with advising and responding to the governors/Board of Management, the principal must establish a constructive working relationship with the unions and professional associations that look after the interests of teaching and support staff. It is wise to acknowledge their legitimate role (as well as its limits) early on in consultations about policies and plans, especially if these have a potential impact on workload, customary practices or job security. Treatments of controversial issues and of particular disputes are rendered at least a little less fraught if there has been a genuine acknowledgement of the rightful place of unions in school life, if principals are able to distinguish for themselves disagreement about specific proposals from personal attack, and if the case put forward by school leaders is made credible, not only in terms of its rationale and supporting evidence, but also because it is made by people who show integrity and honesty, and who have a record of behaviour that demonstrates impartiality between different factions and parties in the school.

If organisations are machines, control makes sense. If organisations are process structures, then seeking to impose control through permanent structure is suicide. The fundamental issue that the education management industry has to grapple with is a confusion between order and control. ...Managers cannot install effective management systems but can intervene in the energetic and creative human interactions already happening around them. Therefore management training and development based on strategies, tools and rational cycles for proactively empowering people is an expensive illusion. (Helen Gunter, op. cit., pp. 91, 102.)

8. PRIORITIES FOR CATHOLIC SCHOOL LEADERS

In this final section I highlight six priorities that I believe should be given emphasis in the political style or thrust of Catholic school leaders. First, if they strive for the development of a strong sense of collegiality among their staff, they will find themselves simultaneously challenging any attempt to withdraw into some form of isolationist autonomy and any tendency to slip into a collectivism that subordinates the individual. Collegiality goes beyond congeniality in that it does not rest satisfied with harmonious relationships and working alongside one another in an easy fashion and in a friendly atmosphere. It demands joint (and costly) commitment to a cause larger than the goals of any particular person and indeed beyond a concern for the survival and flourishing of the whole school community. An emphasis on collegiality reminds us that school can, at most, only ever be a penultimate priority and value for the members of that community. If we acknowledge God as the supreme authority in our lives, we will avoid placing on schools expectations that they are not able to meet. If our hopes rest on God, then the authority of both school and political leaders is relativised, put into a broader perspective and reordered for us as potential avenues for serving the Kingdom. For 'every politics courts idolatry, the displacement of the sovereign God by a sovereign collective societal purpose', and we should remember that 'God sits in judgement over *all* nations, including our own'.[12]

Second, in their use of authority, influence and power, Catholic school leaders should favour trust over control and they should rely more on mobilising people rather than on managing structures. In any dispute, they should be concerned to win people over rather than simply to win. 'Without voluntary interaction, one may have slavery, incarceration, or blind followership, but one cannot have leadership, which never depends upon just force or ignorance.'[13] In the long run, the credibility of school leaders depends less on the information that they have at their disposal, the trappings of office and status that are granted to them, and the 'sticks and carrots' that they are able to offer or to wield, than it rests on the degree of care, commitment, consistency, integrity, openness, transparency and vulnerability that they display in all their dealings. Thus their *modus operandi* will be perceived to match with, indeed, to exemplify, their purposes and goals. They will be seen to be 'walking the talk'.

Third, Catholic school leaders should ensure that their schools are outward-looking, in that the education offered in them builds up in students both a willingness and a capacity to contribute to the wider society, the promotion of justice and the common good. The potential accusation that Catholics, in wanting separate education, are only interested in providing for their own children, must be demonstrably false. The graduates of Catholic schools should care about the state of public education in general and be equipped to belong properly to the polity (with the qualification already noted that this is a penultimate good). One might apply to one's own national context the comment by the Jesuit John Courtney Murray before the Second Vatican Council: 'Each American Catholic comprises a church-state relation. The believer is "church" by participation, and as representing that participation. The same person, who is also a citizen, is the "state" by participation, and as representing a citizen's informed judgement'.[14] In this third priority I am emphasising that the promotion of citizenship is an important aspect of education for discipleship, that engagement with citizenship will modify and enrich one's understanding of what is entailed by discipleship, and that this relationship is reciprocal, in that citizenship itself will be understood more deeply and lived more appropriately if interpreted in the light of our primary role as disciples. 'What citizenship adds to discipleship is: a wider solidarity, a humbler service, a new reality test for responsibility. What discipleship adds to citizenship is: utopia, counterculture, and vocation. …The duties of citizenship protect the church from narrow parochial introspection.'[15]

Fourth, as figureheads of their community, and as protectors of the boundary between school and the external world, Catholic principals should maintain a constant and discerning vigilance with regard to the impact of alien ideologies. The espoused ethos of Catholic schools can be undermined unwittingly by any of the following: the use of new technology, uncritical assimilation of messages from the mass media, bowing to market forces or the adoption of managerialist models. In the face of individualism, materialism, relativism, secularism and scientism, and in response to some forms of pluralism, liberal humanism and technical rationality, Catholic school leaders need to remain alert themselves and to equip their students and colleagues to engage these challenges critically.

Fifth, if they are to work in partnership with the Church, as sharers in its mission, then Catholic school leaders might be expected to make every effort to stay in close contact with the various representatives of the Church, for example, diocesan officers, trustees from religious orders, and the local bishop. Furthermore, they need to familiarise themselves with local, national and international guidance documents that cast light on the purpose and essential nature of Catholic education. Although their school has a particular context, some unique features and its own internal priorities, it should recognisably reflect much in common with other Catholic schools and it should be inspired by a Catholic view of creation, life, learning and community. At the same time, where this is possible, one would expect Catholic school leaders to co-operate especially closely with and offer mutual support for their counterparts in other Catholic schools, seeking to foster a real sense of fellowship among the Catholic educational community. Such a concern for the common good of Catholic education will sometimes entail a degree of self-sacrifice with regard to the apparent interests of a particular school, for example, in the context of diocesan reorganisation. Without this dimension of communication and collaboration with the wider Catholic community, guardianship of the mission *within* a school will be unbalanced, malnourished and incomplete (and therefore neither fully catholic nor Catholic).

Finally, Catholic principals should never lose sight of those who are meant to be the primary beneficiaries of their leadership, the students. 'By its very concept, educational leadership is never primarily for the benefit of administrators, teachers, political groups, or economic interests; it is always mainly for the education of students. Hence the end of educational leadership must embody an idea of what education is and the form that idea will take in the students for whom the leadership is responsible.'[16] Although society (and the Church) grants teachers some authority over students, and principals over teachers, in each case the purpose of such authority is to facilitate the empowerment of others and to create a climate where the invitation to respond freely and fully to the gospel may be heard. However useful the examination of the implications of various metaphors, such as school as family, as business, as Church or as political community, turns out to be for Catholic school leaders, it must not obscure the fact that schools exist for learning. Furthermore, they are places where the promotion of learning is integrally related to living the gospel.

RECOMMENDED READING

Callan, E., *Creating Citizens. Political Education and Liberal Democracy* (Oxford: Oxford University Press, 1997).

Catholic Bishops' Conference of England and Wales, *The Common Good and the Catholic Church's Social Teaching* (Manchester, 1996).

Catholic Education Service, *The Common Good in Education* (London, 1997).

Department of Catholic Education and Formation, *A Struggle for Excellence* (London: Catholic Education Service, 1997).

——*Foundations for Excellence* (London: Catholic Education Service, 1999).

Conroy, J. (ed.), *Catholic Education Inside-Out/Outside-In* (Dublin: Lindisfarne/Veritas, 1999).

Lawton, A., *Ethical Management for the Public Services* (Buckingham: Open University Press, 1998).

McMahon, J., Neidhart, H. & Chapman, J. (eds), *Leading the Catholic School* (Richmond, Victoria, Australia: Spectrum Publications, 1997).

Markham, D., *Spiritlinking Leadership: Working through Resistance to Organizational Change* (New York: Paulist Press, 1999).

Riordan, P., *A Politics of the Common Good* (Dublin: Institute of Public Administration, 1996).

Tuohy, D., *The Inner World of Teaching* (London: Falmer Press, 1999).

NOTES

1. Paulo Freire, *Pedagogy of the Oppressed* (London: Penguin, 1972); see also Freire's last book, *Pedagogy of Freedom* (Lanham: Rowman & Littlefield, 1998).
2. Padraig Hogan, *The Custody and Courtship of Experience* (Dublin: Columba Press, 1995), p. 171.

3. CGCCST, p. 12. The common good is to be seen as 'a guarantor of individual rights, and as the necessary public context in which conflicts of individual rights and interests can be adjudicated or reconciled'.
4. Ibid., p. 8.
5. Ibid., p. 13. Local institutions are to be defended against central ones. Authority should be 'as close to the grass roots as good government allows'.
6. Ibid., quoting Pius XI, (1931), *Quadragesimo Anno*.
7. CGCCST, p. 14. 'This then is not a feeling of vague compassion or shallow distress at the misfortunes of so many people, both near and far. On the contrary it is a firm and persevering determination to commit oneself to the common good'. Ibid. (quoting Pope John Paul II, 1992, *Sollicitudo Rei Socialis*). Solidarity is closely related to Aristotle's description (in his Ethics) of civic friendship. It also echoes Aquinas' treatment of justice as the establishing of a right order in society, one which orients all the virtues. (*Summa Theologicae*, q. 58, art. 6.)
8. CGCCST, p. 3.
9. Ibid., p. 7. Cf. p. 17. '"Common" implies "all-inclusive": the common good cannot exclude or exempt any section of the population.' All should therefore both contribute to and benefit from the common good.
10. Ibid., p. 10. From the right to life flows the right 'to those conditions which make life more truly human: religious liberty, decent work, housing, health care, freedom of speech, education, and the right to raise and provide for a family.'
11. Ibid., pp. 17-27.
12. John Coleman, *Educating for Citizenship* (ed.) Mary Boys, (New York: The Pilgrim Press, 1989), p. 39.
13. Robert Heslop, 'The Practical Value of Philosophical

Thought for the Ethical Dimension of Educational Leadership,' *Educational Administration*, 33 (1), 1997, p. 73.

14. J. C. Murray, quoted by Thomas Hughson in *The Believer as Citizen* (Mahwah: New Jersey, 1993), p. 11.
15. John Coleman, loc. cit., pp. 35, 59.
16. Heslop, loc. cit., p. 74.

CHAPTER SIX

SCHOOL AS ACADEMY

An alternative name for a school is 'academy'. More generally this term indicates that the prime purpose of such an institution is the acquisition of knowledge, the development of learning skills and the capacity to advance knowledge. People who teach in academies are licensed by society; they are recognised as possessing the necessary types, quantity and quality of knowledge that society wishes to be transmitted to the next generation as desirable 'equipment' for its own good and that of the wider community. Such 'academics' are authorised, mandated, and paid to pass on their knowledge. More narrowly, the term 'academy' often, although not always, indicates a focus on the academic, the cognitive and the intellectual dimension of knowledge, in contrast, for example, to the aesthetic, sporting, technical or professional.

When we talk about focusing on the academic, one or more of the following features is often envisaged. First, we might mean a concentration on mental skills, as opposed to physical, social or emotional development; that is, we can imagine a person being academically gifted, but lacking ability in some of these other areas. Indeed, sometimes the word 'academic' is used pejoratively, to imply someone at home with the abstract and with ideals, but with much less facility in dealing with the concrete and the real circumstances of life. Or, alternatively, we might mean the capacity to understand, deploy, enjoy and explain the principles, ground-rules or grammar of a particular activity, even if skilful practice was less evident. Third, we might speak about the creation of an academic 'atmosphere', intending by that term to suggest a context where the imperious and intrusive demands of everyday life, for example, of family or friends, of community membership and of economic necessities, are at least temporarily stilled, or kept at bay, in order for a relatively leisured space to be fostered. Within an academic setting we can review our normal assumptions, reflect on questions about meaning and worth, appreciate pattern, beauty and argument, stretch the imagination and think about possibilities, not being limited to what is present. In this space we can play with language and ideas and experiment with alternative scenarios.

In this chapter the term 'academy' is used in the limited sense of being a place set aside for the purpose of promoting students' learning. I postpone until section two the question of which type of learning this might be. It will be an integral part of my argument that, in order to function as environments that foster learning, schools must also be places that are for students, and more demonstrably so than hitherto.

In this chapter I first underline the centrality of learning as the major priority within schools and suggest that this centrality is sometimes threatened by displacement activities or competing priorities. Second, I indicate how the curriculum is contested, as much in Catholic schools as in others. Third, the diverse senses in which classrooms are contested areas are brought out. Fourth, I explore what is meant by providing hospitable spaces in school, spaces that provide the kind of atmosphere that is conducive to learning in general and to an education that is both Catholic and catholic. Finally, some of the connections between Christian teaching and Christian learning are indicated. Such connections rest upon the mutual bearing on one another of classroom practice and school ethos, the impact of moral and spiritual qualities on intellectual growth (and vice versa) and the ongoing formation of teachers and their sense of vocation.

1. The Centrality of Learning

In reading educational management literature, or in attending in-service courses that concentrate on developing or enhancing leadership skills and competencies, it is easy to forget the absolute centrality of learning as the principal task of schools. The promotion of students' learning is the first and overriding priority in a school. By comparison, other concerns should be very clearly subordinate: the budget and the bureaucracy, meetings and marketing, strategic and development plans, inspection and appraisal, hierarchy and authority, even protection of the rights of staff to decent pay, promotion prospects, satisfactory working conditions or consultation. These things matter, of course, in the sense that, without them, schools are likely to lack both efficiency and humanity. They help to provide the foundation on which a house of learning might be built and they are part of the superstructure supporting its effective maintenance. However, all these things do not supply the *raison d'être* for a school, which is simply to be a place that is organised in such a manner that it facilitates and fosters, elicits and encourages, learning by students.

Although the overriding importance of promoting student learning in schools should be so obvious that it does not need articulating, nevertheless, in practice, it can certainly seem to students that schools exist primarily for the sake of teachers; while for many teachers it can feel as if schools exist primarily for the sake of a variety of other groups, for example, parents, or administrators, or the State, or the economy, or society in general. In the case of Catholic schools, it can also seem as if the school exists primarily to serve the Church. Although in a sense this is true (see chapter four), such service of the Church, if it is carried out too imperiously, brooking no debate or room for differences in interpretation, can sometimes appear to function as a partial turning away from, or perhaps even a distortion of, the particular needs of students. In this chapter I take the view that if schools are to have any chance of treating the promotion of learning as their principal goal, then it must become more apparent to students that schools exist above all for them. This does not imply that schools should care any less than they do now for truth or for tradition; neither does it mean that they should be ready to accommodate each and every wish of students or capitulate to their diverse desires. Such a strategy would be self-defeating and would in fact contribute to the obstruction and undermining of learning. However, it does mean that great efforts are made to ensure that schools take students and their perspectives seriously and that hospitable spaces for learning are created for them.

Another way of setting out my purposes here would be to describe them thus. First, we need to restore a proper sense of priorities within schools, so that all activities are embarked upon and all systems are constructed in service of learning. Good teachers have never lost sight of this; they have never let themselves be deflected from this goal in the deployment of their energies. However, this goal is not as straightforward as it may at first appear, for there is controversy within society as to what kinds of learning are of most value. I shall touch on this in the next section, devoted to 'contested curriculum'. My intention here is simply to acknowledge the prospect, if not the actual occurrence, of a significant displacement of energy in the face of the increasing number of advisers and inspectors, of agencies and authorities, of representative boards and consultative bodies, which have steadily accumulated around the work of schools, demanding that ever greater attention is given by school leaders to policy documentation, to audits of value for money, and to proof of progress. It is little wonder that sometimes principals feel that they are rapidly losing touch with the unpredictable drama of classroom exchanges and with the personal encounters to be experienced there.

Second, in the context of Catholic schools, I wish to support the growing recognition that such schools should endeavour more explicitly to combine inclusiveness with their distinctiveness, so that their curriculum is more catholic as well as Catholic. Sadly, not enough of our students have felt that deep sense of acknowledgement and acceptance, of warmth and belonging, of trust and of being taken seriously, that one might hope would be features of any healthy educational environment. My credo as regards inclusiveness has three closely connected dimensions. First, I believe that a failure to be inclusive (in the sense of catholic) in curriculum matters impoverishes the educational programme of students; it leaves out important aspects of life. Second, a failure to be inclusive (in the sense of multidimensional) in pedagogical methods undermines the capacity of students to engage positively with learning; it relies on too narrow a range of teaching styles and approaches to learning. Third, an unwillingness to be inclusive (in the sense of warm and welcoming) in classroom relationships and atmosphere inhibits, if it does not cripple, the willingness of students to risk committing themselves to the uncertain business of tackling new topics, fresh material and unfamiliar tasks.

My treatment, in chapters two to five, of school as family, as business, as Church and as political community, did not rule out the role of schools as centres of learning. Indeed, a great deal of important learning takes place in families, in businesses, in Churches and in both politics and the community. But in those chapters the focus was mostly on features other than the deliberate and explicit promotion of learning.

Of course, no model can stand in isolation from all the others. Thus, in the family context – that is, in the home and in the familylike dimension of school – one must attend to the 'business' dimension, if one is to pay one's bills in the present and to secure the future. The Christian family constitutes a 'domestic Church', an entry into the life of faith (or unfaith) and the earthly soil in which our understanding of sacrament and grace can be fertilised or frozen. It is also in the family that we come to an early sense of the use and misuse of power, influence, bargaining, exchange and co-operation in the pursuit of interests and goods. When it works well, the family gives us such a strong sense of identity and belonging, of worth and self-confidence, that we are willing to risk new experiences and be open to learning from the university of life.

Likewise, in the world of business, considerable emphasis is given to investing in people as our primary and most valuable resource. There, too, stress is also put on fostering a sense of belonging and loyalty, at least to a small degree, in order to replicate some familylike features, to make room for intimacy and to reduce anonymity within large-scale organisations. There is, in many businesses, as much reference to mission statements (corporate goals), to ethos and to service, as we hear in any other sector of life. To this extent, at least, a business can reflect some Churchlike features. The world of business both demands and develops many political skills, in the jockeying for position, in mobilising support for a proposal, in the determination and cunning required in seeing off opposition. Much time, energy and creativity, as well as money, is devoted in many businesses to lifelong learning and ensuring the constant development of new skills, in order to remain competitive and to preserve one's leading edge in the market.

In the ecclesial world, too, great emphasis is often given to fostering a feeling of family, for instance at the level of the parish, among the members of a religious order and between the clergy. In its local, diocesan, national and international expressions and organisations, there is plenty of scope for businesslike administration and the deployment of management skills. Notoriously, the Church has always been bedevilled by the intrusion of the political. The requirement for Church leaders, at local level and beyond, to learn and to display political skills, is no less today than it was in the past. Such political acumen is needed in dealing with the mass media when they seek to highlight scandal, disaffection and disagreement among Church members. It is called for in responding constructively to growing diversity at all levels within the Church. It has always been a vital survival skill in the slipstream of the kind of turbulent relations between centre and periphery that have always prevailed in such a large international community.

If the title most often attributed to Jesus in the New Testament is 'Teacher', and if the Church is charged with conveying the gospel to all people, then education will always be at the very heart of her mission. Christians believe that the Holy Spirit is always calling us forward into new aspects of salvific truth and into new understandings of how our lives can be more deeply converted towards God's ways. This belief should keep the Church in learning mode. As became clear in chapter four, recent developments in ecclesiological thinking, for example, an about-turn in seeking a positive relationship with the world, together with a deeper appreciation of the notions of *sensus fidelium* and of reception as elements within living tradition, jointly result in a renewed understanding of the Church as a community of learners. This new emphasis serves to counterbalance an earlier predominance of the idea of the Church as teacher. Teaching and learning are as intimately connected in the Church context as in any other.

2. CONTESTED CURRICULUM

A curriculum can be considered from several angles, for example, the explicit content to be covered in courses, the processes involved in teaching and learning, the kind of environment created, and the purposes that permeate the whole effort. I focus on the last aspect, since this will colour all the others.

Many purposes and priorities compete for attention, time, resources and acceptance within a school curriculum. Both continuity and change among these priorities can be recognised. Should learning focus more on understanding, appreciating and using appropriately the natural world? Or should it prepare us to enjoy eternal life by prioritising the spiritual dimension within education? What is the relative importance we should give in schools to promoting the capacity for independent judgement as compared with co-operation? Should schools give most of their time to equipping students to take their place in a rapidly changing, technologically advanced economy, or should they concentrate more on developing the kinds of qualities and skills required for participation in a pluralist, democratic society? Do we want to encourage wealth-producing, entrepreneurial, market-oriented and computer-literate potential employees who can advance our country's share of the world economy, or should we instead give high priority to citizenship and community building? What is the relative importance we wish to attribute to self-assertion as opposed to self-denial? How much is it the role of schools to promote learning about the body, emotions, personal relationships and self-knowledge? What about those domains of knowledge that deserve attention for their own sake, the sciences, the arts and the humanities? And, issuing directly from an acceptance of the gospel, where do we place an option for the poor in relation to all these other priorities within schools? What kinds of knowing do we seek to encourage in schools and what difference do we hope such knowing will make in the lives of students, both now and in the future?

In an article, 'Converting the Baptised', published in
America in 1989, William O'Malley SJ picks out five
things we should teach: (1) to be aware and curious; (2)
to be humble and honest in dealing with data; (3) to
think logically, thoroughly, open-mindedly and
accurately; (4) to care about one another; and (5) to
stand up and be counted.

Throughout history there have been many goals for
schooling. [These goals may be listed as:] conveying
information, usefulness, saving one's soul, physical and
moral discipline, vocational education, formation of a
'lady' or 'gentleman', training of patriotic citizens,
promotion of national ideals and culture, students'
psychological development, creative expression,
conformity with the findings of science, adaptation of the
individual to the constraints of society, social efficiency,
and preparation for the reconstruction of the social order.
(Harold Buetow, *The Catholic School* [New York:
Crossroad, 1988], p. 77.)

Buetow (a) identifies many of the 'isms' that are available in the
cultures surrounding Catholic schools and (b) picks out from
one leading Christian thinker (Thomas Aquinas) some topics
that we can expect will have a bearing on a Catholic
understanding of and approach to education (p. 66). With
regard to (a), he lists pragmatism, empiricism, positivism,
secularism, naturalism, materialism, atheistic existentialism,
and Darwinian evolutionism. Insofar as these offer ways of

interpreting life, they have the potential to provide frameworks for and priorities within a curriculum. With regard to (b), among his suggestions are truth, human intellectual powers, free will and choice, habits, love, fear, virtue, and our last end or destiny.

1. Pick any three from (a) and show how they might influence the curriculum in ways that are not in harmony with a Catholic perspective.

2. Pick any three topics from (b) and show how a Christian understanding of these suggests a different view of human nature from some of the "isms" listed in (a), and then bring out the curriculum implications if the three you select were taken seriously as guiding principles in Catholic schools.

3. "Given that Catholic education must continue to be in the world whilst not necessarily *of* it, the promotion of 'citizenship' must form part of the life and mission of Catholic education." What are the implications of this statement for curriculum development in your school?

4. (a) In what ways do you think that the 'basics' in education – in terms of knowledge, attitudes, skills and understanding – in the twenty-first century will differ from those in the twentieth century? (b) Which changes in the next twenty-five years – ecclesial, economic, environmental, political, scientific/technological and social – are most likely to impact upon education and how?

5. What can you guarantee as an educational entitlement for *all* students in your school at the present moment? (c) What would a survey of current practice indicate that you could

not yet guarantee for all students, but that you think you should be able to raise to the level of such a guarantee within three years?

6. Are there ways in which our current approaches to (i) the deployment of teachers, (ii) the allocation of time, (iii) access to learning resources and (iv) modes of assessment might be made more flexible in order to promote student learning more effectively?

7. In looking ahead to the curriculum of the future, which of the following four questions do you find most interesting and fertile for new thinking: (a) *What* will we learn? (b) *How* will we learn? (c) *Where* will we learn? (d) From *whom* will we learn?

---

8. Do some subjects have a higher status than others for students? What evidence do you have for this? What influences students in the way they view different areas of the curriculum? Is it any different for teachers or for parents? (Adapted from David Tuohy, *The Inner World of Teaching* [London: Falmer, 1999], p. 117.)

---

9. A number of questions can be asked about curriculum proposals: (i) Says who? (ii) On what grounds? (iii) How do we know this? (iv) Who will benefit from doing things this way? (v) Who will lose? Select any two of the following areas of recent curriculum proposals and then apply the questions above to them: (a) numeracy; (b) separate subject work in junior schools; (c) citizenship, (d) separate sciences; (e) vocational education in school; (f) health education;

(g) education for personal relationships; (h) foreign languages in primary/secondary schools.

Schools should produce young people with ideas and dreams, with a vision of what they want to achieve in life, who have a strong sense of service of care and compassion for those in need, and who have above all a love of life, a zest for living life to the full. (Cardinal Basil Hume, 'Profession and Vocation: Teaching in the Third Millennium', address given 18 March 1999 to the Churches in England Joint Conference.)

How different should the curriculum be in a Catholic school? Some teachers imagine that the answer to this question comes down to a privileged role for religious education and a protected space for worship. Clearly such an answer is inadequate.

The separation of forms of knowledge and increasing specialisation has led, according to Robert Davis, to a gradual confining of the Christian elements to specific areas of the curriculum (in Conroy, 1999, p. 216). Davis argues (p. 222) that Catholic schools have paid a price where they have sought secular accreditation and public funding – the restriction of Catholicity to religious education, ethos and worship. This, together with other changes in Catholic higher education caused by social and cultural trends, has led to an abandonment of the kind of integral humanism advocated (originally in the late 1930s) by Maritain. Since the Second World War and particularly since the Second Vatican Council, the Catholic Church has moved away from the kind of separatist existence, in parallel with the State, that prevailed in many (non-Catholic) countries for much of the earlier part of this century. Greater openness to society and an emphasis on positive engagement and dialogue with the world has led, not only to acceptance, but even to assimilation, of the Church.

Davis emphasises the importance of relating the content of every part of the curriculum to a coherent Catholic philosophy of education. He stresses the need for schools to give as much energy to the application of this philosophy to each of the subject areas as they have expended in recent years in the construction of a Catholic ethos. He argues (p. 226) for a 'dynamic affirmation of the truth claims of Catholic anthropology, shared in charity, humility and dialogue with the surrounding polity', being confident that this can be carried out while avoiding 'any suggestion of academic surveillance or exclusivity'. If this Catholic philosophy of education can be re-appropriated by teachers, it is more likely that they will be able to bring out the 'adversarial potential' (p. 227) of the curriculum. Such a counter-cultural witness is required if Catholic education is to be true to itself and if it is to serve the common good.

10. In what ways, if any, do you consider that your school curriculum functions, at least partly, as a counter-cultural witness?

A major reason for the existence of Catholic schools is to ensure that the wholeness or integrity of Catholic education is preserved. Central to this wholeness is the principle of the non-separation of sacred and secular in learning and throughout the curriculum. This principle is founded upon the belief that, neither in the person of Christ, nor in the sacramental nature of reality, is there any separation between the divine and the human. So, too, in the experience of our lives, we should not expect any divorce between nature and grace. It follows from this principle that the curriculum in a Catholic school should demonstrably be one that is marked by a high degree of integration and interconnectedness across its many elements. A recent authoritative document from Rome challenges Catholic schools to put more emphasis on the importance of interdisciplinary studies and interconnectedness as essential features of the curriculum.

The General Directory for Catechesis, issued by the Congregation for the Clergy at the end of 1997, reiterates the importance of interdisciplinary dialogue in Catholic schools and suggests that such dialogue should be prompted by religious instruction. 'In this way the presentation of the Christian message influences the way in which the origins of the world, the sense of history, the basis of ethical values, the function of religion in culture, the destiny of man and his relationship with nature, are understood. Through interdisciplinary dialogue religious instruction in schools underpins, develops and completes the educational activity of the school.' (p. 74).

Although the essential interconnectedness of all areas of knowledge (and therefore the desirability of interdisciplinary work) has always been compatible with Catholic principles, it has not always been given strong emphasis alongside some of the other elements that have an enduring place within the Church's educational philosophy, such as religion as the core of the curriculum, Christ as the model for human life, the Church as the medium of living tradition that cannot be bypassed, the spiritual dimension of life to receive due attention, morality to be seen in objective terms and mortality to be kept in view. While both Newman and von Hugel in the past and, more recently, Kevin Nichols, have staunchly advocated the need to keep always in mind the interconnectedness of knowledge, this is not a refrain much reflected in curriculum practice. In the light of the Directory's comment, perhaps teachers of different curriculum areas should expect their work to be receptive to the religious atmosphere and worldview on which the school is founded. They cannot claim to be uninfluenced by it.

I wish to draw attention to the significance of interconnectedness, as a renewed emphasis within Catholic educational principles, for four reasons. First, the particular form of a belief system's interconnectedness will have implications for the kinds of education that belief system seeks to foster. Second, it is the belief in the *essential* interconnectedness of the various elements of Catholic education that leads to a desire on the part of the Catholic community to establish and maintain separate schooling, rather than to provide *additional* teaching of those elements that have not been covered in mainstream schooling. One might claim that neither the explicitly religious nor the apparently secular can be properly appreciated if taught in isolation from the other. Third, without an emphasis on interconnectedness, some of the key elements within Catholic education (highlighted above) could be distorted. Fourth, although the Directory's underlining of interdisciplinary dialogue builds upon ideas about the role of Christ in our lives and also relies upon the notion of shared values in a school's ethos, it goes beyond these in respects that have implications for curriculum planning and classroom practice.

It is communion with Christ that is meant to give all the various activities of school a coherence and their special religious tone. At the heart of Christian faith is the belief that 'in Christ all things hold together' (Col 1:17) and that therefore a Christian should 'take every thought captive for Christ' (2 Cor 10:5). Relationship with Christ requires radical conversion in our thinking and lifestyle, without which we cannot appreciate the salvation he offers. 'The unspiritual man does not receive the gifts of the Spirit of God, for they are folly to him, and he is not able to understand them.' (1 Cor 2:14).

I take this to mean first, that Christ is to be of paramount importance in the life of a Christian, second, that through relationship with Christ a believer will find that all things will 'make sense', but only in the light of a continuing process of conversions in our thinking and lifestyle, and third, that in the context of Catholic education it is appropriate to consider the relevance of the teaching and example of Christ for all aspects of knowledge and action.

It is sometimes hard for outsiders to appreciate that, in the context of Catholic education, this special perspective means more than simply a feature to be added to what would otherwise be a standard educational programme, for example, more time for specific religious teaching, or more frequent occasions of collective worship. All the various elements within education, as the (English and Welsh) bishops' 1981 report, *Signposts and Homecomings*, indicated (p. 121), are affected by its focal point, its leading principle, its special perspective: 'curriculum, syllabus, discipline, systems of reward and punishment, worship, relationships, community, catechesis.'

Chesterton recognised that, according to its own logic, Catholic theology would be all-pervasive in a school following a Catholic conception of education; such theology could not be taught for only part of the time, in separate packages labelled religious education, and then hidden away or left on one side. As he said, 'every education teaches a philosophy; if not by dogma then by suggestion, by implication, by atmosphere. Every part of that education has a connection with every other part. If it does not all combine to convey some general view of life, it is not education at all' (G. K. Chesterton, *The Common Man*, [London: Sheed and Ward, 1950], pp. 167-8). This was as true for the Catholic as for any other approach to education.

Therefore, not only will religious teaching be distinctive in Catholic education, but many other aspects of school life are expected to reflect Catholic principles or priorities, for example, sex education, teacher appraisal, pupil assessment, parental rights and relationships with the local community. Teachers should take care, however, not to impose an integrating framework that is so strong, it inhibits pupil initiative.

There is also an interconnectedness between what is frequently understood to be the enduring four dimensions within Catholic education: its interpretation of its central message, the kind of community it seeks to be, the nature of service to be fostered and the worship to be offered. Each one of these four requires the assistance of the others; each one will have repercussions on the others. What Chesterton in his essay on Catholic education called atmosphere or environment is sometimes spoken of as 'permeation'. This would include both the explicit and the hidden curriculum, as well as extra-curricular activities, the school's social arrangements for staff and students and the methods used to evaluate progress towards carrying out the school's mission.

This notion of permeation flows from the central importance given to religion within a Catholic school and from the belief that religion should both affect and be affected by all aspects of human formation. Von Hugel insisted that the religious dimension of life can attain its greatest richness only when all other aspects of human life are equally well developed. Any omission, imbalance or exaggeration in one area of study will have repercussions elsewhere and will certainly undermine religious maturity and well-being.

The advocacy of permeation is at the same time a refusal to accept any rigid or permanent compartmentalising of school life, for example, into secular and religious spheres. No ultimate separation between what might be called sacred and what might be called profane can be sustained. What is being looked for is a *synthesis,* where the Christian perspective is neither merely *juxtaposed* – simply put alongside of a secular curriculum – nor *superimposed.* Any attempt at theological imperialism, where all aspects are taught under the direction and scrutiny of religious principles, is a misinterpretation of the nature of the synthesis envisaged. Study of secular realities is not to be adulterated by nor subordinated to contact with a religious perspective on life that is all-consuming, suffocating, distorting or constricting. Nor is religion itself to be absorbed within a secular worldview: the transcendent should not be described as if it refers merely to the term of our continuing and natural development, thereby being rendered as immanent.

I am qualifying here the notion of the autonomy of the disciplines, not in service of any theological imperialism, which is always to be resisted, but in acknowledgement of God as the source and goal of all truth, in allowing for the limitations of human penetration of truth, and in recognition of the complementarity of various perspectives on truth. Several implications follow from such a view. First, the methodology and findings of any particular discipline are to be considered, despite their construction by human 'instruments' or agents, as potential avenues towards an understanding of God's purposes for us, rather than merely as serving purposes we have arrived at for ourselves. Second, we should, in due humility, allow for the tentativeness or provisionality of the knowledge we think we have arrived at, this being as true of claims to religious knowledge as of any other kind. Third, the findings of one discipline are best appreciated in the light of complementary knowledge provided by other disciplines; none (including theology) is adequate on its own. The totality of disciplines together constitutes a circle in which each one conditions, frames, challenges and illuminates the others.

The major agents of the interconnectedness of a Christian worldview will surely be teachers who personally exemplify congruence between content, methodology and lifestyle and who embody a harmony between the life of faith and the pursuit of academic study. Any attempt to bring a transforming Christian perspective to bear upon an area of academic study needs the personal example of teachers to give it purchase and credibility and to make it sufficiently attractive to be worth serious consideration by pupils. At the same time it has to be admitted that over-reliance on the good example of teachers, without the attempt to bring a Christian perspective to bear upon and to transform the disciplines, fails to engage with academic subjects adequately and leads to a juxtaposition between, rather than a synthesis of, faith and culture.

Such a view of the seamless web or the total interconnectedness of Catholic education is not new. In his *De Doctrina Christiana,* Augustine had said that 'all subjects [must] be surveyed in the light of being connected with one another, and they cannot be understood except in the light of those interconnections'. A Catholic philosophy of education should promote among a school staff a concern for maintaining a unified approach to and vision of the educational enterprise. It should help them to avoid incoherence in the curriculum and fragmentation in the pursuit of separate spheres of knowledge, but it should combine this with a degree of sensitivity to the respective jurisdiction and scope of the various subjects within the curriculum. Perhaps one beneficial way of engaging with their mission for a Catholic school staff on an in-service day would be to reflect upon this fresh challenge to establish the right connections and to explore its professional and personal implications.

11. How comfortable are you and your teaching colleagues with the notion that the Catholic school curriculum should be marked by a high degree of interconnectedness and that

it should encourage interdisciplinary enquiries? What kind of safeguards or assurances might some colleagues need in the face of possible concerns about 'theological imperialism' or religion dominating the curriculum, distorting what is taught, or undermining the necessary autonomy of different subject areas?

3. CONTESTED CLASSROOMS

The classroom has always been, to some degree at least, a contested arena. There are several dimensions to such contests. Here I focus on five aspects. First, there is an encounter, sometimes amounting even to a clash, between two worldviews: that of the more and that of the less educated. The perspective of the learner, in relation to what is to be learned, is limited in at least some respect by comparison with the more augmented viewpoint of the teacher. Often this encounter between people possessing different amounts of knowledge with regard to a particular topic also turns out to be one between people at different stages of life, between those who are older, more mature and experienced, and those who lack these advantages.

Second, any classroom exchange, if it is to be fruitful, usually requires some form of accommodation between the requirements of the curriculum and assessment, the variety of learning styles preferred by students and those methods that form part of a teacher's 'repertoire'. This accommodation will be arrived at either through negotiation or through imposition, perhaps even through accident or serendipity. Curriculum requirements and their associated assessment systems are usually set up at a distance from a school; they are meant to be relatively impersonal and universal. They set out expectations and standards that necessarily do not envisage particular people and local circumstances. But in the practice of teaching, some kind of compromises are called for. Perhaps part of the curriculum receives less attention or a different kind of treatment than that originally intended, either because students are not interested in it or because teachers feel unfamiliar with it or simply take the view that there are other priorities. Perhaps students have to be inspired, or enticed, tricked, encouraged, or sometimes compelled, to tackle subject matter or to engage with learning methods that they find uncongenial, uninteresting, irrelevant or even alien. Teachers, too, have to adjust, as they find that some of their approaches meet too much resistance to be worth persisting with, or that some methods are barren, or that new techniques are called for. Inescapably, at every level of education, an effective classroom is a place that requires a sensitive and precarious balancing act between the nature of the material to be learnt, the needs of learners and the preferences of teachers. This is as true of postgraduate work as it is in the nursery. In this contested site or arena for accommodation, all the 'elements' are in a state of flux, owing to the huge changes going on in society and in schools. Therefore any accommodation reached at a particular point can only be provisional and tentative, to be re-established tomorrow or in another classroom.

Third, the classroom is also a contested site in the sense that all students are competing, either actively or by implication, for the attention and support of the teacher. Yet their learning needs differ enormously. Some students start with significant advantages, impressive social skills, high levels of confidence, and positive support from home. Others lack all of these. We are more aware than ever of some of the obstacles to learning that have to be negotiated by teachers and the factors in schools and classrooms that can hinder progress. Among these might be included innate impairment or disability, linguistic difficulties, cultural factors, gender issues, illness, dysfunctional families, poor teaching, peer-group pressure, emotional disturbance, lack of study skills or simply lack of access to learning resources. The kind of contest going on in a classroom in the face of all of these factors will depend partly on the sensitivity of the teacher, in 'reading' or registering all these diverse needs, and partly on the desperation of students and their capacity to call for help.

Fourth, classrooms are places where there is a contest for control, order and discipline. One of the earliest concerns of a teacher is the establishment and maintenance of good order, without which learning is impossible. If the teacher is insecure, lacking in confidence, ill at ease, or feeling threatened, then students have little chance of the optimum conditions for their learning to be created, even if they appear to revel in the teacher's discomfort. Disruption, bad behaviour, excessive noise, unpredictability cumulatively undermine the leisured and open space and risk-taking required if learning is to be nurtured. The battle for control is not one just for the teacher, however. I intend to bring out in section four, below, how optimum conditions for learning also require some sense, on the part of each student, that s/he exercises at least a degree of control, discretion, or room for manoeuvre. Without the possibility of initiative on my part, as a learner I cannot properly appropriate what is being taught; it cannot become 'mine'.

Finally, there is another sense in which a classroom is a contested arena. Various 'technologies' or media compete for dominance. There are many different resources and modes of communication available in the classroom that students are expected either to attend to or to employ. These include the teacher's voice and physical presence, the role of print, in the form of textbooks and handouts, the use of black- or white-boards. Then there will be discussion, writing, computers (for word-processing, CD Roms, and accessing databases and the internet), television and video-recorders, radio, audio-tape, movement, and, whether legitimised or not, the place of touch and gesture. Both at home and at school, students are more and more able to communicate with greater rapidity, with more people, over greater distances and with regard to exponentially increasing areas of knowledge than ever before. The balance between what must be learned in school and what can be learned elsewhere is rapidly changing, as are the kinds of questions that can be posed. Changing technology imports different worldviews and new priorities (including, for example, the need for media literacy to have a high profile as an accomplishment of the educated person).

4. HOSPITABLE SPACES FOR LEARNING

Despite the inevitability of the classroom being a contested arena, it is the task of the teacher to turn this situation around so that it can also become a hospitable space. A hospitable space is one where we feel invited and welcomed, recognised and known by name, safe and comfortable. In such an environment we can relax, be ourselves and enter into reciprocal relations with others. In the midst of co-operation, the individuality of all is protected. We feel addressed in conversation and capable of responding. Teachers cannot expect to be heard if they are not prepared to listen to what students have to say. If we are conscious of compulsion, hostility, judgement, rejection or threats, then our self-defence mechanisms leap into operation and we prepare to fight or flee, or if that is not possible, then at least we get ready to hide, to withdraw, to close down our vulnerability.

A classroom atmosphere that facilitates learning will be one in which there is a reluctance to label anyone too definitely, for this can lead to self-fulfilling prophecies and can foreclose on our options. A hospitable classroom leaves all parties room for manoeuvre and allows them a high degree of flexibility of response. We do not always have to act in the same way or at the same speed. If it is to prompt learning, then the hospitable classroom will appear to us as a place that offers both challenge and support.

Here I refer to four writers who have recently commented eloquently about the need for schools to become more hospitable places for students. The first of these is the American psychologist James Day, who emphasises the role of relationship and commitment as key ingredients in education (in Conroy, 1999). This relationship and commitment have to be established with other people, students and teachers, and with the object of study. But the quality of personal relationships in the classroom has priority for Day, in the sense that, without a positive experience of this, the student cannot give herself properly to any area of study. Elements contributing to positive relationships include self-esteem, mutual respect, trust, confidence, integrity, realism, humility and a sense that we count and can make a difference. In an earlier essay, Day has shown the devastating effects on learners when they feel sacrificed on the altar of truth and personally mutilated in the name of moral correctness (in McLaughlin, O'Keeffe and O'Keefe, 1996). After experiencing such inhospitable classrooms, students have to spend a long, painful time unlearning the pedagogy of estrangement.

The second writer on a similar theme that I wish to draw upon is the Irish philosopher of education, Padraig Hogan (Hogan, 1995). Hogan advocates a type of education that does not seek to exercise control over students, but rather one that is a form of 'courtship'. Learning becomes hospitable when it uncovers each student's unique identity and promise (p. 151). A teacher has to *appeal* to students' attention, efforts, commitments; s/he cannot *command* these, for as soon as this happens, their ownership disappears, like gold being transmuted immediately into lead. Only with the right form of address, one displaying an appropriate 'courtesy' and invitational tone, will the emergent abilities and sensibilities of students resonate with authenticity and integrity.

Hogan outlines (p. 171) the educational virtues required of teachers if schools are to offer hospitable spaces that release and enable learners:

(a) a circumspect honesty in declaring one's own intentions as a teacher;

(b) patience and persistence, which are adroit rather than importunate;

(c) the courage, the moral energy, and the perseverance to tackle challenges and obstacles;

(d) frankness, coupled with respect for each student's privacy and dignity;

(e) an originality, which resists the ruts of habit and returns ever anew to the address of the subjects which are the teacher's abiding point of contact with the students;

(f) a judicious faith in students, even in unpromising circumstances;

(g) a disavowal of proprietorial designs, coupled with a constructive sense of self-criticism;

(h) a categorical sense of care for students as young human beings, recognising the claims of both equity and difference, and with unfailing expectations as a key ingredient.

The third writer on this theme to be mentioned here is the recently retired teacher/educator from Durham, England, Robert Graham. His sensitive and moving book of reflections on experiences in teaching and learning, *Taking Each Other Seriously*, reiterates my plea for schools to function as hospitable spaces for learning and it offers many examples of what this might entail. It also provides plenty of evidence of the harm done when learning is expected to occur in a cold emotional climate, one that is unappreciative of and even blind to what the student brings into the classroom from his/her own experience. He refers to teachers 'in whose company students felt they could really be themselves' (p. 26), to places that 'cater for a lot of you functioning' (i.e. they encourage you to articulate, rather than hide, many of your real feelings and views) (p. 80), and to institutions whose inhabitants 'feel potentially whole and known', rather than 'fragmented and missed' (p. 82). He rightly claims that 'we do our best learning from positions of hope and faith, rather than scepticism and distrust' (p. 121). If we are listened to with respect, if our experience is accepted as valid, worth hearing, and even of significance, then we can put more of ourselves forward willingly into the otherwise vulnerable and frightening unknown space just ahead, where learning takes place.

Fourthly, from the field of spirituality, the Dutch writer Henri Nouwen explicitly describes (in *Reaching Out*) the type of inclusiveness to be exercised by teachers within the classroom as 'hospitality'. Such hospitality creates a free and friendly space that allows students to grow and it reveals to them that they have something to offer as well as to receive (p. 81). Nouwen invites teachers to think of their students as guests in their classrooms, guests who need affirmation, encouragement and support, but also a degree of unambiguous confrontation and challenging witness from the teacher. 'Receptivity without confrontation leads to a bland neutrality that serves nobody. Confrontation without receptivity leads to an oppressive aggression which hurts everybody' (pp. 91-2). Nouwen's emphasis on 'hospitality' as an aspect of the teacher's role implies neither paternalism nor any failure to recognise the importance of encouraging student 'ownership' of their classrooms; although it does suggest that the primary responsibility for developing this rests with the teacher, especially with younger students and in the context of compulsory schooling.

Nouwen's sense of hospitality entails an invitation to students to share their experiences, insights and questions. It implies an acceptance of such contributions as gifts to be welcomed, respected and valued. But it goes beyond this, to offer an encounter, through the teacher, with the insights and values of another world, one that transcends that which is currently envisaged by the students. If the teacher is to reach out to students, starting from where they are, if s/he is to 'embrace' their needs, to accept their concerns and perceptions, nevertheless s/he is not to leave them at this point but instead to encourage them to 'travel' further.

The teacher, who knows the subject well, must introduce it to students in the way one would introduce a friend. The student must know why the teacher values the subject, how the subject has transformed the teacher's life. By the same token the teacher must value the students as potential friends, be vulnerable to the ways students may transform the teacher's relationship with the subject as well as be transformed. (Parker Palmer, *To Know as We Are Known* [San Francisco: Harper and Row, 1983], p. 104.)

---

12. What is your response to this notion of teaching as being in some respects like friendship? What benefits might there be from adopting this notion? What limits should

there be? What will influence our capacity to be 'appropriately vulnerable'?

13. What can teachers do to ensure that they are 'fired up' by, are enthusiastic about the curriculum areas they teach? If what we are teaching hasn't made a big difference to us, should we be teaching it?

14. In what senses does teaching students of any age require an atmosphere displaying both hospitality and tact? In your response imagine you are faced with someone who is sceptical about the key notions suggested on this page and cynical about either the necessity or the possibility of there being such a thing as a spirituality of teaching.

15. Be ready to share with your study group anything you have come across that has contributed to or influenced your own 'spirituality of teaching'.

If Catholic schools are to reflect the gospel theme of ministry to the outsiders, the poor and the rejected, then hospitable spaces for learning within them must be offered not only to the devout and the committed, but also to those on the margins of acceptability, the semi-committed, the half-believers, the occasional participants, and the lapsed or 'resting' Church members. Those who are deviants, sinners, unorthodox, unpopular, unsuccessful, disabled, that is, the poor, interpreted broadly, all can potentially benefit and contribute. Students with learning difficulties and behaviour problems, those who are non-conforming, critical or dissenting, all have an important part to play in a Catholic school. If a Catholic school is to be true to its gospel roots, such students should experience acceptance and affirmation as persons with an inalienable dignity. Their uniqueness should be cherished, their talents nurtured, their questions taken seriously, their capacity for redemption never lost sight of, nor their spirits crushed. This does not mean that bad behaviour is condoned, explained away, ignored or downplayed; nor does it mean that the school should not strive for worldly success in terms of examination passes, sporting results, entry of students into higher education or into a variety of vocations. But it does imply that the schools should seek to treat these aims as subordinate to other goals, ones that relate more directly to the spread of the gospel, acceptance of its message, and furtherance of the Kingdom of God.

16. Try to give a realistic indication of the range of answers that might be given by teachers with curriculum leadership responsibilities in your school to the question: 'how is what we are doing affecting the poor?'

> How does the preferential option for the poor affect each of us in our respective disciplines? Is making this option a strictly private matter? Does it have any bearing on fields apart from religion and social ethics? Does language about the preferential option belong more properly in the chapel than in the classroom? ...Is there a way of teaching or communicating to students the profound human sensibility which underlies the choice to align oneself with the poor? ...Does the option for the poor require that the very way we conceive the subject matter of our studies has to be transformed? ...Is education capable of being an instrument of social justice? ...How do we advocate the option for the poor within an educational institution without seeking to impose it? (William Reiser SJ, *Love of Learning: Desire for Justice* [University of Scranton Press, 1995], pp. 6, 7, 9.)

One way in which Catholic schools demonstrate their commitment to the Gospel is through the inclusion of people with disabilities. ...It has been estimated that, nationally, some 20% of the school population will have Special Educational Needs... which includes children with physical, behavioural, emotional, sensory and learning disabilities, at some stage in their school career... Our growth as the body of Christ is linked inextricably with being an inclusive and enabling Church. (Bishops' Conference of England and Wales, *Valuing Difference* [London: Catholic Education Service, 1998], pp. 50, 14.)

17. What kinds of issues arise for your school in responding adequately to the needs of the disabled – with regard to (a) teachers, other staff and governors; (b) buildings and accommodation; (c) learning resources; (d) family support?

Effective learning takes place in the zone between comfort and panic, in which a learner is engaged and stretched, but not beyond her capacity to adapt and to incorporate new information and insights. (Tom Bentley, *Learning Beyond the Classroom* [London: Routledge, 1998, p. 62.)

18. Which of the following has been most influential in your own learning: (a) family; (b) classroom/school; (c) work/apprenticeship; (d) leisure?

19. (a) How would you describe the way you teach and how would you describe the *rapport* that you establish with students?

(b) Why do some students learn more in some lessons than in others? What are the student-related factors that are operative?

(c) Why are some lessons more effective than others? What are the classroom-related factors here?

(d) What can be done to enhance *collaboration* among teachers in your school?

Many institutional factors seem to have a bearing on the quality of learning that is possible in a school. These operate at a different level from those factors that are student-related (for example, the natural capacities with which they have been endowed, their motivation, efforts, past experiences, their study skills and home support). They also have an effect that supervenes on the work of individual teachers. These institutional factors can either undermine or reinforce the efforts of students and teachers.

I pick out six examples of institutional factors that impact upon learning, only commenting briefly on some of them. First there is the timetable, which includes considerations of how lessons are scheduled, their duration, frequency, timing, sequence. One might enquire here into the degree of flexibility possible and, indeed, who decides this. Second, there are decisions at school level about how students are allocated to particular classes or groups. Here one might question by what criteria, in what mix of composition and number and for which purposes they are so grouped. Third, the school's behaviour policy will set parameters within which both teachers and students will have to work. Fourth, the kinds of accommodation available, in terms of appropriateness for facilitating different types of learning, comfort and space, for example, as well as outside-of-lessons arrangements, cannot help but make a difference positively or negatively. (Can the students stay indoors without supervision? Are the toilets acceptably clean and safe areas or are they danger-spots for students and is their smell repellent?) Fifth, the availability of sufficient learning resources will often be beyond the control of individual teachers or students. Sixth, the degree to which the staff work collaboratively as a team, or merely as a collection of individuals, is likely to be at least partly due to the way they are managed. Students quickly become aware of the possibilities of playing off one teacher against another, or of seeing cracks within the system if there isn't consistency among teachers with regard to approaches to discipline and to work.

20. Which one of these six institutional factors bearing upon learning would probably benefit most from further attention in your school at this moment?

The teachers who inspired and helped us were surely nearly always the ones who took us seriously, who believed in us and gave us a stronger sense of our own self-worth and potential. (Cardinal Basil Hume, 'Profession and Vocation: Teaching in the Third Millennium', address given 18 March 1999 to the Churches in England Joint Conference.)

21. Research on human learning suggests a close connection between *emotional climate* and effective learning. To what

extent can, *should* and does your school encourage students to express their feelings as well as their 'higher-order' thinking?

Key Principles identified for school approaches to differentiation in *Differentiation: a Catholic Response* (London: Catholic Education Service, 1997). Every learner:

- has a divine origin and is a unique individual;
- is gifted by the Holy Spirit;
- has the right to be included fully in the life of the Church community;
- has the right to education and to have potential identified and developed;
- has the right to be regarded as having equal value and worth;
- has the right to a broad, balanced, relevant and differentiated curriculum;
- has the right to genuine access to the whole curriculum;
- has the right to be challenged by and to achieve in the learning situation;
- has the right to share with and learn from others.

The role of teachers is described by Tom Groome (*Educating for Life*) as having five aspects: (a) designing an environment; (2 providing a language; (c) sharing resources; (d) questioning assumptions; (e) modelling creative fidelity to tradition and critical openness from it.

In the worlds of work and relationships, we are beginning to understand that high performance flows, not from the rigid imposition of external structures and constraints, but from the distribution of responsibility and a commitment to honesty, transparency and shared goals. When these conditions are met, the true constraints on performance and fulfilment begin to appear, and the means to overcome them can be created. (Tom Bentley, *Learning Beyond the Classroom*, op. cit. p. 4.)

5. CONNECTIONS BETWEEN CHRISTIAN TEACHING AND CHRISTIAN LEARNING

How might one go beyond description of such hospitable spaces and relate these to the fostering of a Christian school ethos? First, we might claim that teachers who provide such hospitable spaces for learning are offering a great gift to their students, something precious, and that is themselves. Each teacher is an expression of one of God's gifts intended for the benefit of students. Insofar as each teacher is different, then her or his particular gift cannot be offered by anyone else. The more of themselves that teachers share, the richer students will be.

Second, by imparting their subject or curriculum expertise, a teacher opens up the world as seen from a particular perspective. By breathing life into this subject area, a teacher makes it a possible vantage point from which to see the world. Catholic teaching respects the relative autonomy, subject to the Lordship of Christ, of each of the disciplines. We can find something special, valid, useful and enriching through every one of the areas of study.

The important principle of the autonomy of the disciplines is held in creative tension with the belief that we should seek to provide and to model a synthesis between faith, life and culture. Without distorting the subjects we teach, it is possible, *through them*, to open up perspectives on God's world, people, purposes, call and grace. The teacher's task here is to help students find connections between those aspects of their experience and study that can be described in secular terms and the language and worldview that flow from the perspective of faith. I have already commented on interconnectedness (in section two). At this point I merely wish to emphasise that the clear compartments or labels we use in classifying types and sources of knowledge are for convenience, in order to make reality manageable for us at any particular moment. From a Christian perspective, there is no separation between the secular and the religious curriculum; there is no more separation between the divine and the human in our lives or in school learning than there is in the person of Christ. God is as close to us in the laboratory, sports field, playground, classroom, library, workshop and cloakroom, as in private prayer, public worship, the words of Scripture and sacramental practice, although, on our side, we may be less aware of that presence.

What might be the role of a teacher who seeks to be sensitive to the spiritual dimension in any particular curriculum area and to promote the spiritual development of students in the course of their work? I pick out several generic qualities that could apply across the curriculum, although they would be given practical expression in different ways, according to the nature, methods, priorities and opportunities of each subject area.

First, the teacher would be able to identify some mind-boggling questions, ones for which s/he doesn't know the answers or at least lacks certainty and must remain tentative. These should emerge from the discipline or topic of study. Second, s/he will be aware of some of the answers that others have given to these questions. Third, s/he will be conscious of the limits of such answers. Fourth, s/he demonstrates an awareness of the limits or boundaries of her/his particular curriculum area, as well as familiarity with its basic assumptions and essential foundations. Fifth, s/he will model for students what it means to be a person with an open mind, able to live with uncertainty and ambiguity. Sixth, s/he will have some settled dispositions and at least some provisional convictions about the journey of life, although still able to revise these, if necessary, in the light of further experience and fresh evidence. Seventh, s/he will exhibit a 'space-making' ability, facilitating others in their questioning and reflection on the spiritual, in the midst of other aspects of learning.

A teacher who possesses these qualities is well on the way to allowing the classroom to function as a holy place. Such a teacher does not forget that students are whole people, even as s/he is dealing, at a particular time and place, with a narrowly prescribed skill, or a particular notion, or a small drop in the ocean of knowledge. The lives of students are multidimensional, with unforeseeable reverberations potentially sparked off in any compartment of their being by an apparently mundane aspect of learning. Even an arid exchange in a classroom can stimulate something vital within the student, without the teacher ever being aware of this; at the same time, even the most religious subject matter can leave a student unmoved and be experienced as a spiritual desert. We can make the classroom a holy place by the way we try to meet students' needs, by the quality of the relationships we establish with them, by our hard work, regular and punctual attendance, by our thorough and conscientious preparation and planning, by our marking of work and assessment of progress, and, above all, by our readiness to listen. Our own good example, our enthusiasm, our combination of challenge and support, together with the way we model collaboration with our colleagues – all these help towards making classrooms holy places.

The principles and approaches that make classrooms hospitable spaces for learning are particularly necessary if such classrooms are ever to have the potential to become holy places for students with long-standing 'wounds'. I provide below two extended quotations from a priest who has carried out extensive work with children and young people in care. These extracts bring out powerfully the depth of suffering that some students bring to school, the kinds of obstacles to learning that these burdens constitute and the type of response called for if schools are truly to be *for* learners and if they are to offer hospitable and healing spaces that foster holiness. They also provide encouragement for teachers, showing that practices such as collective worship can make an important and positive difference in the spiritual development of such students.

1. If a child or young person has been abused, demeaned, neglected and made to feel worthless, he or she may find it very difficult to trust – let alone love – another person, especially another adult. They may have a tendency towards isolationism. They will need understanding in their human spirituality.

2. If a child or young person has had no contact with religious faith, if religion has always been ridiculed at home, or worse, if the young person has prayed for some abuse to stop and the abuse has continued, then the meaning and truth of worship may be very difficult for them to come to terms with at all. They will need understanding and support in their devotional spirituality.

3. If a child or young person has had a highly dislocated and problematic background, then he or she may find it very difficult to build up a coherent and cohesive interpretation of life. There may be a tendency towards

dislocation and fragmentation in thinking and a degree of the erratic in behaviour and relationships. They will need understanding and support in their practical spirituality. (John Bradford, *Caring for the Whole Child* [London: The Children's Society, 1995], p. 68.)

22. How do you offer opportunities in school for such students to build up a sense of trust and consistency?

1. For pupils who are in care, either in a foster or residential home, school worship can be a treasured moment of looking beyond their own immediate circumstances, and of being uplifted by a sense of the Divine and by the challenge of the adventure of life as a whole.

2. For the pupil whose life has been significantly disturbed or disrupted by the illness of a parent or by bereavement, by the divorce or separation of parents or by the long-term absence of (or even the lack of knowledge of) a parent, school worship can offer a serious and neutral place where, privately, a prayer can be said for those secretly most dear.

3. For the pupil who suffers pressure, unpredictability and disruption at home, school worship can be an oasis of peace, an experience of fraternity and an expression of 'order'. God can be met as the One who brings both outer harmony and inner stillness.

4. For the pupil who has suffered victimisation or abuse and who has a very low sense of self-worth, or who has low self-esteem for some other reason, school worship can be a time of reassurance and encouragement through the collective celebration of God's love and concern for

each individual – not just for the 'top scorers', the 'best lookers' or the group-leaders. (J. Bradford, p. 58.)

23. Which parts of your school's work seems closest to having this kind of effect on students who have suffered a troubled history?

24. Which has been most influential in your own religious learning: (a) belonging to a faith community; (b) prayer; (c) care for the needy; (d) the preached word; (e) receiving specific religious teaching; (f) your own experience of teaching?

The degree to which the curriculum is Catholic, the level of permeation of gospel values through everything that happens will depend not on what is written on paper but what is in the hearts and minds of the people who are charged with the ministry of its practice. The real curriculum is determined by the nature and commitment of teachers in the context of their classrooms. (Source not traced.)

The presence of good and holy teachers does not guarantee that goodness and holiness will be learned; there are counter-teachings always present. However, the absence of good and holy people does guarantee that goodness and holiness cannot be learned. (Maria Harris and Gabriel Moran, *Reshaping Religious Education* [Louisville: Westminster John Knox Press, 1998], p. 33.)

25. As you reflect on your memories of your own education and your experience of teachers in your current school, what is your response to the comment above?

The life of the Catholic teacher must be marked by the exercise of a personal vocation in the Church…. [For this to remain alive and active] religious formation must be broadened and be kept up to date, on the same level as, and in harmony with, human formation as a whole…. [Evidence of the fruits of this vocation will be] professional commitment; support of truth, justice and freedom; openness to the point of view of others; combined with an habitual attitude of service; personal commitment to the students, and fraternal solidarity with everyone; a life that is integrally moral in all its aspects…. [As for the virtues required of the teacher,] faith is the unfailing source of the humility, the hope and the charity needed for perseverance in their vocation. For every educator is in need of humility in order to recognise one's own limitations, one's mistakes, along with the need for constant growth, and the realization that the ideal being pursued is always beyond one's grasp. Every educator needs a firm hope, because the teacher is never the one who truly reaps the fruits of the labour expended on the students. And, finally, every educator is in need of permanent and growing charity, in order to love each of the students as an individual created in the image and likeness of God. (*Lay Catholics in Schools: Witnesses to Faith,* The Sacred Congregation for Catholic Education [London: Catholic Truth Society, 1982], 37, 62, 52, 72.)

26. In what ways do you/can you provide your staff with the encouragement that will nourish their sense of vocation?

> God's real presence in the educational process is manifest not primarily as subject of a particular discipline but in a particular attitude toward learning as a whole.... One of the main objectives of the Catholic school [is] to *de-religionize* our faith by extending the religious attitude beyond the limits of sacred doctrine to all areas of existence. Religious education should provide the stimulus to reflection in wonder on all reality. (Louis Dupre, 'Catholic education and the predicament of modern culture', *The Living Light*, 23 (4), 1987, p. 303.)

27. What are the obstacles to as well as some prompts for the development of such a religious attitude toward all areas of our experience?

> Scholarship from a religious perspective can be considered as enquiry into the ultimate nature and purpose of God's creation. 'To understand things is to realize the relationship they have to Christ.' (Jean Leclerq, *The Love of Learning and the Desire for God*, p. 39.)

> [Some people operate on the basis of] the principle of the empty head, [which assumes] freedom of intellectual enquiry from all prior assumptions about nature, the world, human society, and God. (Bernard Lonergan,

> *Method in Theology* [London: Darton, Longman &
> Todd], p. 156.)

Inevitably, religious beliefs will colour and shape for us those things we study. Our motivation for scholarship, the questions we pose, the assumptions we rely upon, the significance that we attribute to our findings, the larger framework of meaning we draw upon in order to relate new ideas and insights to our previous understandings – all these will be modified if we dwell in (and therefore 'look out from') a life transformed by religious perspectives.

Furthermore, in recent years there has been a growing appreciation of the degree to which our growth in knowledge is dependent upon the kind of person we are becoming. Our moral, spiritual and intellectual development is inextricably interconnected. The darkness of the mind is related to the darkness of the heart. Our relative closeness to sinfulness or to sanctity has cognitive implications. 'How we think, and what we choose to make the major preoccupations of our minds throughout our lives, determine a great deal of what we become' (Denise Lardner Carmody, 1996, p. 182).

Moral and intellectual virtues mutually reinforce each other, while their counterparts mutually ruin one another. Some of the intellectual qualities that make learning possible, for example, inquisitiveness, teachableness, attentiveness, persistence and circumspection, themselves depend on a moral component, as becomes clearer as soon as we identify those intellectual vices that obstruct learning: obtuseness, gullibility, close-mindedness, wilful naivete and superficiality of thought (W. Jay Wood: *Epistemology: Becoming Intellectually Virtuous* [Leicester: Apollos, 1998], pp. 35, 47). Even the word 'thoughtful' connotes something moral as well as mental, as does its opposite, 'thoughtless'; we refer by these terms both to the presence or absence of a quality of thinking and of consideration for others. If we are to think well, we must live well; and vice versa. 'If we fail to oversee our intellectual life and cultivate virtue, the likely consequence will be a maimed and stunted mind that thwarts our prospects for living a flourishing life' (Wood, p. 17).

Thus, the formation of minds transcends the academic; it is an endeavour that is inseparable from spiritual and moral development. Humility, faith, self-denial and charity are virtues that (separately and conjointly) exercise a considerable influence on the possibilities of growth in knowledge. Humility opens up room for learning from the presumed authority of a teacher, text or object of study. Faith prompts us to rely upon and to trust others, to step out in the risk-laden venture that any learning entails. Self-denial gives us the capacity to abandon those views or practices that threaten to prevent further learning or recognition of the truth. Charity encourages us to put the best construction on an interpretation of some phenomenon, engages us in a sympathetic relationship with the object of our study and allows us to come close to it without threats to its nature or distortion of its functioning.

If school is to be an academy, a place where learning can flourish, then teachers have to cultivate in themselves as well as their students those moral and spiritual qualities that make possible the life of the mind. They also have to demonstrate that school is a place that is genuinely concerned to put students first. If they succeed in this, they will have created a true ethos, a hospitable space, for enquiry. A double commitment has to be shown by teachers, to a universal 'message' and to the particular person that each student is called to become. Such a double commitment, to learning and to learners, should facilitate both a powerful witness in the service of truth and a willingness on the part of students to respond wholeheartedly and positively.

There are many who seek knowledge for the sake of knowledge: that is curiosity. There are others who desire to know in order that they may themselves be known: that is vanity. Others seek knowledge in order to sell it: that is dishonourable. But there are some who seek knowledge in order to edify others: that is love. (St Bernard of Clairvaux, in the twelfth century, quoted in Mark Schwehn, *Exiles from Eden* [New York: Oxford University Press, 1993], p. 60.)

Education is an essentially religious activity, with a religious object as the ultimate referent (truth, goodness, beauty, holiness, eternity, divinity) and a religious power or agent as the ultimate teacher [the divine or God]. Religion is concerned with those events, practices, and beliefs that form the root or boundary experiences of life, the points at which the fundamental mystery of life itself is most deeply encountered. Along with birth, growth, achievement, decline, and death, education is such a root experience. (Peter Hodgson, *God's Wisdom* [Louisville: Westminster John Knox Press, 1999], pp. 2, 5.)

Catholic intellectual traditions offer a standpoint outside of the conventional wisdom of academic disciplines, a well-thought out and carefully articulated alternative perspective from which the contemporary researcher can criticise effectively the limits imposed on thinking by axioms underlying work in a field. (James Turner, 'Catholic intellectual traditions and contemporary scholarship', *Catholic Education*, vol. 2, no. 1, 1998, p. 41.)

The academic and the religious are intrinsically related, they form an inherent unity, [and] one is incomplete without the other.... The Catholic university knows that religion does not substitute for the sciences and arts. Physics does not become theology and business is not piety; law remains forever itself and mathematics has its own autonomy. Faith and culture are distinct, but not separate. In the university they are united but not identified. What the Council of Chalcedon said of the humanity and divinity of Christ can be said of faith and culture as components of the Catholic university in a highly analogous fashion: one is not to be confused with the other; one is not to be changed into the other; they are not to be divided off from one another; they are not to be separated from one another. It is their individual integrity that allows for them to be united rather than identified. [For 'university', read 'curriculum'.] (Michael Buckley, SJ, *The Catholic University as Promise and Project* [Washington, DC: Georgetown University Press, 1998], pp. 15, 18.)

RECOMMENDED READING

Bayliss, V., *Opening Minds: Education for the 21st Century* (London: The Royal Society of Arts, 1999).

Bentley, T., *Learning Beyond the Classroom* (London: Routledge, 1998).

Boys, M., *Educating in Faith: Maps and Visions* (San Francisco: Harper & Row, 1989).

Carmody, D. L., *Organising the Christian Mind* (Valley Forge, Pennsylvania: Trinity Press International, 1996).

Congregation for the Clergy, *General Directory for Catechesis* (London: Catholic Truth Society, 1997).

Conroy, J., (ed.) *Catholic Education Inside-Out/Outside-In* (Dublin: Lindisfarne/Veritas, 1999), chs 9 and 12.

Graham, R., *Taking Each Other Seriously* (Fieldhouse Press, University of Durham, 1998).

Grenier, B., *Jesus the Teacher* (Homebush, Australia: St Pauls, 1995).

Groome, T., *Educating For Life* (Allen, Texas: Thomas More Press, 1998).

Himes, M., 'Catholicism as integral humanism', in *The Challenge of Pluralism* (ed.) F. Clark Power and Daniel Lapsley (University of Notre Dame Press, 1992).

Hogan, P., *The Custody and Courtship of Experience* (Dublin: Columba Press, 1995).

McLaughlin, T. H., O'Keeffe, B. & O'Keefe, J. (eds), *The Contemporary Catholic School* (London: Falmer, 1996).

Nouwen, H., *Reaching Out* (London: Collins/Fount, 1980), ch. 5.

CHAPTER SEVEN

CONTRASTING POLARITIES

In this chapter I explore two different but overlapping polarities, both of which have a bearing upon the contested nature of Catholic schooling. First, there is the polarity between objectivity and subjectivity in religious education and in the wider curriculum. Second, there is the polarity between teacher and student as centres of initiative in classroom communication.

In the case of the first polarity, I assume that we all inhabit simultaneously two worlds, one within and one external to us, though these worlds are not divorced from one another. Our access to both the inner and the outer world requires the capacity to analyse and to synthesise our experiences. It also depends upon the capacity to receive as well as to contribute. Perhaps it would be more accurate to claim that the (one) world can be explored in two broadly different ways, one being objectively, the other being subjectively. The first considers things as they are in themselves, while the second considers things as they relate to us. Neither makes adequate sense without the other. The fruits of a judicious combination of objectivity and subjectivity in education should include, on the one hand, realism and relevance in the curriculum, and, on the other hand, well-stocked and agile minds among students who are both formed and transformed by what they learn. Without these features, Catholic schools would be much the poorer.

In the case of the second polarity, I suggest that a deeper penetration of the complex relationship between teaching and learning can be achieved by combining the retrieval of a particular interpretation of rhetoric with a renewed commitment by teachers to allow a pivotal role for judgements made by students. Rhetoric, as understood by Aristotle, correlates message, speaker and audience in the subtle and sophisticated art of moral persuasion. In the context of school, an application of Aristotle's use of rhetoric turns our attention to the complex relationships that exist between the teacher as medium of communication, the content to be communicated, and the students as the 'target' of such communication. A focus on the rhetorical dimension of teaching emphasises the importance of credibility and trustworthiness more than it does knowledge or authority. A focus on judgement then turns our attention to the need to stimulate independent, critical thinking on the part of students and the exercise by them of a more active role in the classroom. Judgement has a crucial part to play in building the self, but because it makes us confront the question of truth, it helps us to keep in constant contact with reality. Without judgement we do not come to own what we have learned. The fruits of a judicious combination of rhetorical skills by the teacher together with the provocation of judgement by students can be expected to include a positive, trusting and active engagement with teachers, learners secure in their own identity and integrity, and a creative and responsible appropriation of tradition. Without these features, Catholic schools would find their mission an impossible task.

1. Objective and Subjective Approaches

Underlying many of the discussions about religious education there seems to be an uneasiness about the relative weight to be attached to an objective or to a subjective approach to the subject. This is so no matter which aspect of the process is under scrutiny. People feel uncertain with regard to, for example, the status of the knowledge purveyed in the classroom, or how amenable the language and concepts are to children's understanding, or how well-matched the content of a lesson is to the emotional development and cultural situation of young people.

Some teachers concentrate more on a factual method, where accuracy, comprehensiveness and justice are key criteria by which to measure one's teaching. Here scrupulous attention is given to detail, to the avoidance of anachronism and stereotyping, and due note is taken of the multidimensional scope and internal diversity of a religion across time and culture. The phenomena of world religions are in this way suitably deployed by the teacher. This could lead to a type of knowledge where students come to 'stand over' what they study, rather than to understand it, to have sympathy for, or to show interest in the purposes and feelings of people practising religion. Their engagement with religion may be so clinical and detached that the power of religion to attract or to repel, to mobilise human effort and to maintain it in the face of defeat and disappointment, may escape them altogether, or at least be rendered as innocuous, insipid or even incredible.

Other teachers put their efforts into a subjective approach, one that focuses more on the aspirations, fears, strengths and weaknesses of learners, one that is more concerned with their 'inner' world than with imparting knowledge about those living religious traditions of the world outside us. Yet this can cause students to lose out in important ways. It is possible to explore, express, share and celebrate personal concerns, but still to neglect that widening of horizons stimulated by contact with what is other, strange and foreign to us. Students can be parochial about time and culture if we allow them too easy a concentration on the prevailing ethos and immediate needs thrown up in one's classroom. An inward-looking isolationism and ignorance about what has been treasured by millions of believers within the world religions will impoverish the lives of students.

We all inhabit simultaneously two worlds: one within and the other external to us. The degree of our understanding of the outer world is dependent upon the richness of our internal development. For example, a study of those answers to human problems enshrined in the religions cannot be effective if we pay no attention to the degree to which pupils consider the questions themselves as worthy and the problems to be pressing. However, our inner development is closely related to the contacts we make with what is external to us, causing us to modify, little by little, our own perceptions and priorities.

Religious education, like all education, oscillates between these two worlds. Lack of balance is often one factor responsible for the apparent failure of education. Sometimes such failure is attributed to unsatisfactory content, or to inappropriate methods, while, at other times, inadequate contexts or insufficient resources are made to take the blame. I think, however, it relates to that uneasiness mentioned earlier, about where to place the weight in religious education. This needs to be seen in the wider setting of the dialectic between subjectivity and objectivity that should pervade the whole educational process. How are we to view the tension between these two, and what does it mean to aim for a healthy balance that includes both?

In education, we cannot afford to sacrifice either the development of a critical intellect or the nurturing of a creative imagination. One-sided emphasis on the former can lead to scepticism about truth, coldness in relationships, isolation from tradition, relativism with regard to values, a sense of superiority over other creatures and a willingness to manipulate nature as our servant. It could evoke neither compassion nor devotion. Too much emphasis on the creative imagination, however, can cause students to lose touch with reality, and their teachers might fail to inculcate those skills necessary for participating at any level in the academic traditions that encapsulate current knowledge and ways of adding to it. Such skills include awareness of the criteria by which it may be possible to check, verify or refute truth-claims. It can lead teachers and students to expect a flowering of knowledge and achievement without sufficient attention to their roots. Undisciplined enthusiasms are usually short-lived, infertile, unbalanced and unreliable. Children need something to be critical with, material on which their imagination can play, and equipment and training in its use, dangers and limitations, before being let loose on the world. (I include material and conceptual equipment here.)

Analysis aids us in taking something apart to see how it works, while synthesis is the art of putting together elements that at first sight are disparate. Synthesis is not mere aggregation or addition, for it involves a personal contribution, linking together the parts that have been collected into a new whole. Analysis and synthesis should be attempted together at all stages of education. The two approaches to the material of learning are both vital, since analysis puts us in touch with reality, while synthesis ensures that we are not merely operatives, fitting into a system that is already fixed by nature. We need to be not just instruments for a society that is pre-ordained; but rather actors, independent originators, capable of new initiatives.

Analysis, which must be objective, and synthesis, which requires subjective involvement to some degree at least, can be combined as a two-fold operation that is applied to a wide range of objects in learning. The process is as relevant to studying a play, a poem, a picture, a picnic-table, a language, a period of time, as to our knowledge of places, procedures and techniques, even traditions, whether they are social, political, cultural, moral or religious. Understanding on its own is insufficient, although absolutely necessary, for without it we are doomed to be at the mercy of the hidden persuaders who can manipulate and control us. Nor is simple imitation of what has been analysed in the course of study, whether this is true, good or beautiful, enough of itself, for the way of imitation leads to a fossilisation of what is fine and impedes progress. Above and beyond understanding and imitation, essential though they both are, we must add the element of contribution; that is, students should put themselves into what they study and make a difference to it, even if at first this difference is only marginal. The object of their study should somehow be enriched by their involvement.

Let me explore a little further this contribution that students can make. I am not thinking of a clear addition to the sum of knowledge in a particular area, nor of a startling new interpretation of it, although both of these are possible, even if rare. Rather I am thinking of a much more modest contribution, one that is nonetheless real and not to be neglected. When teachers face a new class, they begin a fresh journey of discovery together with their students. The topic of study may be new territory for students at the same time as it is familiar ground for teachers, but for teachers, too, the lessons on that topic can be a journey of discovery because of the insights and questions, the mistakes and misunderstandings of students. These challenges will force teachers to clarify their ideas, their presentation and their methodology. In the process of engaging with a topic, students will in some aspects of it confirm what their teachers already knew. Yet in other respects they will persuade teachers to look at the evidence again, to reconsider the normal answers when hearing fresh questions, to reframe the concepts employed, to find new applications for them or to notice new difficulties in their use.

From a faith perspective it seems that a combination of the subjective and the objective approaches to knowledge is essential. Only by employing both these ways will we do justice to the inner and the outer aspects of religion. Those features of our inner existence that we experience as a thrust from below, as inarticulate and never fully satisfied yearnings and desires, need to meet and be matched with those features of the external world that we experience as confronting and addressing us. If the 'solid food' of sound teaching is to satisfy the 'stomach' of learners, then we must help students to recognise some of their hopes and desires as the expression of a deep hunger; otherwise they will miss the message and fail to be nourished by it. A concentration on the subjective side of education creates an inner space, awakens the interest of students and prepares in them an active receptivity.

Attention to the objective aspect of knowledge, on the other hand, helps students to recognise whatever they encounter, to see it for what it really is, in both its familiarity and suitability for meeting their needs, but also in its otherness and in its resistance to manipulation. A concern for the objective nature of whatever is being studied (let us call this topic X) expresses itself as the desire to engage whatever X is in itself that is available for all, rather than merely what it might mean to me. An objective approach enables X to be communicated, since it can be shared as something that belongs to no one particular perspective. This last point is important, for none are privileged in getting access to this otherness, nor can it be dismissed as the result of wishful thinking or private fantasy: its public features can be communally explored, encountered, even dwelt in.

Furthermore, to advocate a combination of subjective and objective approaches to study is the only way to allow the 'objects' of study to become, where appropriate, 'subjects' in their own right, where they interrogate and challenge, illuminate, inspire and 'get through' to us. Our knowledge of other persons, for example, depends not only on our openness to and attentiveness towards them, but also on their allowing themselves to be known. They must be willing to co-operate, by taking down the barriers that prevent us from invading their inner sanctuary. Their capacity to be vulnerable, to be patient of investigation and interaction, is a necessary condition of our learning from them, as well as about them. Similarly, my willingness to display this kind of openness and vulnerability and my readiness to reveal more of myself to others in the face of questioning, is encouraged when I know that my conversation partners are sympathetic to and interested in me. It is inhibited when I know that they are so swallowed up by their own personal problems that they cannot properly hear and accurately assess my outpourings.

My advocacy of the combination of objectivity and subjectivity in learning is especially relevant to reflection upon God's inner and outer word to us. People who are so wrapped-up in themselves in a private subjectivity that they are inattentive to, uninformed about and unskilled in interacting with their environment, will fail to see the footprints of God's presence in the sands of their lives. This is how I would express this: the inner melody we hear in some important way needs to be such that it is capable of being in harmony with the underlying symphony of creation, a creation that is uncovered by science and revealed by Scripture. There cannot be a private mysticism ultimately, because this mysticism must be compatible with metaphysics and a morality; how we 'read' reality, behave with others and relate to God must somehow be brought into close relationship and interpenetrate each other. If this 'dovetailing' of our thinking, this integration of our knowledge, does take place, then we can consider ourselves as shepherds of nature and shapers of our environment, as in our participating in society and responding to God as children and friends.

If we maintain a true balance and a creative tension between the subjective and the objective emphases in education, students will be more likely to have some purchase on their knowledge. Then they have a chance of viewing their knowledge as a personal possession, an inward endowment, one that is coherent, significant, relevant to the world they encounter, and efficacious in helping them to respond to it appropriately. The hard-edged analysis and scrutiny afforded by objective study will lead them to recognise an exterior world, one that requires modification of our existence, and restraint and respect, if we are to live in harmony with it. It will lead them eventually to make judgements that can constitute fixed points in the whirling constellation of events, judgements that can provide firm foundations for their negotiation of their surroundings, natural and artificial. It will also make teachers and students conscious of the finiteness of our knowledge, the precariousness of their certainties, the provisional nature of our hypotheses, wherever the evidence seems not to warrant absolute convictions.

If an objective approach makes it possible to exhibit firmness, so that we are not just victims of pressure, subject to the changing tides of public opinion or the pull of personal preference, so too the subjective approach facilitates our willingness to be flexible and open. A proper concentration on the subjective approach, if it stresses our emotions, our imagination, our creativity and our individual perspective, should encourage students to become subjects in their own right, endowed with dignity, capacities, powers and initiative. Then they will be capable of contributing constructively to the traditions and systems already built up, rather than slipping into being objects of the education process, operating by imitation in a closed system. By being 'subjects' they will be the more ready to allow their education to be a transforming experience, rather than one that merely equips them for a fixed world but leaves them essentially unchanged. In other words, they will allow themselves to be altered by what they learn; it should not remain external to them but become part of them.

So often in education our best endeavours seem to meet defeat. Either we doubt the quality of the material we put before our students, or we doubt their ability to benefit from it. If we can ensure that students experience in all areas of the curriculum a creative tension between the objective and the subjective approaches to learning, this may help us to diagnose where we are going wrong at a particular point in the process and to readjust accordingly.

2. FROM RHETORIC TO JUDGEMENT IN EDUCATION

The second polarity to be explored is that between teacher and learner. There is disagreement in educational discussion, as to whether we should focus more on the teacher or the learner. Will educational improvements come about if we are more teacher-centred or more learner-centred? Is this question just about a matter of emphasis, or is something of fundamental importance, at stake, such as an adequate understanding of what is meant by teaching and by learning? I intend to contribute to this discussion by analysing two terms, these being rhetoric and judgement, which cast some light on what is involved in teaching and learning. First, I will argue that there are many similarities between the qualities that are part of effective rhetoric and those that lead to effective teaching. I then compare some features of the act (and the art) of judgement with the promotion of learning, suggesting a close connection. For the purposes of this chapter, I intend to take the rhetorician as an example of a teacher, even though it must be acknowledged that many rhetoricians have non-educational purposes in mind when they pursue their art. It must also be granted that many teachers employ methods that do not look like or depend upon rhetorical devices and skills.

2.1. From Trust to Risk

Rhetoric, or the art of persuasion, is usually thought of as essentially a form of effective transmission or one-way communication. Somebody embodies the art, or at least demonstrates the skill, of so conveying a message that others come to accept it as true, important, worthy of their attention, perhaps even of their commitment. Enquiry into this art of persuasion might then focus on the particular skills and personal qualities that comprise such persuasiveness. In the context of school, we might ask, how can we identify the effective teacher, one who attracts the 'vote' of attention from students, secures their concentration, makes accessible an item of knowledge and persuades them to engage with it in some way, perhaps through application or assimilation.

Judgement, on the other hand, can be considered part of the art of critical thinking. It is something students have to 'do' with regard to the item of knowledge or the topic of study that is offered for their scrutiny. A teacher who wants to bring about a serious examination of a topic might aim to stimulate or provoke judgements about the sources of knowledge, about the processes involved in accessing and deploying it, or about its significance. Getting students to become critical thinkers is usually part of a move away from an emphasis on content in the curriculum; content can rapidly become outdated, whereas skills and processes can be applied to new questions, contexts and circumstances. Becoming critical is also part of becoming more independent, relying less on the authority of the teacher.

If we want to get students to the stage where they are both able and willing to engage in judgement in a serious way on a particular topic, they must be encouraged to rise up from a passive stance in the classroom, put themselves forward and take risks. People usually need persuasion and encouragement to take risks. Such persuasion and encouragement are part of the teacher's role in facilitating learning. This requires the creation of those hospitable spaces described in chapter six. But if there is to be any intrinsic connection between teaching and learning, that is, if teaching is to be more than simply the occasion when or the setting in which learning takes place, then it must envisage an active role for students. There must be the possibility that the application of methods of study and the rules or criteria originally offered by the teacher can be exercised in a way that differs from the teacher's exemplification of them. It might even be the case that a more radical replacement of these methods, rules or criteria is called for in the light of changing circumstances and requirements. To branch out in some direction, to pursue a line of enquiry requires, at least temporarily, the employment, or the modification, of some method that has been borrowed. 'Try this out', the teacher might say, 'see where it takes you'. It seems that there is no getting away from the fact that, in the move towards independence in learning, we often start from trust in teachers and in their methods. Rhetoric, in the Aristotelian sense in which I am using it here, includes the notions of not abusing hearers, of being credit-worthy and of eliciting trust. Without this trust in teachers, there will no real risks taken by students.

2.2. Pejorative or Positive Terms?

Rhetoric is often treated as a pejorative term, implying shallowness on the part of the speaker, distortion of truth and manipulation with regard to the audience. This pejorative interpretation of rhetoric suggests mere cleverness rather than sincerity in the use of words. It implies that speakers bypass or treat as of little account the critical faculties of audiences in the drive to enlist their support for a cause rather than that they aim to stimulate a self-aware and sharply honed judgement. Rhetoric sometimes is associated with an empty claim, something that cannot be substantiated, or with idealistic aspirations that are removed from reality, or with high-blown language that seeks to persuade by appealing to deep-seated hopes and desires that escape the grip of reason. In the same way, the phrase 'teacher-centred' is sometimes treated as if this implied an attempt to dominate in the classroom, a desire to give priority to tradition, a lack of concern for the perspectives, interests and capacities of learners, and the inculcation of passivity and conformity among students.

Critical thinking and student-centred education, on the other hand, are often treated as positive terms, combining the benefits of being simultaneously democratic, innovative and inclusive. Yet in reality, critical thinking can be used destructively as well as creatively and student-centred classrooms can pander to the trivial as well as to the worthwhile. Each can reinforce elitism and conformity. At the same time, both rhetoric and teacher-centred classroom activity can be morally worthy endeavours that allow for individuality, diversity and experiment.

2.3. Correlative Terms

A better understanding of rhetoric and of judgement would cast light on the relationship between teacher-centred and student-centred education, which are more closely related than is sometimes realised. To anticipate my comments below, on the one hand, rhetoric does pay attention to audiences and learners; it does not imply one-way transmission. On the other hand, critical thinking starts with and works on what is first received, and operates via 'canons' and criteria that at least originated from the teacher or tradition. Quinton (1992) and O'Hear

(1992) bring out very clearly how tradition plays an absolutely crucial role in providing a foundation for any creative thought and they show that tradition need not inhibit the development of personal perspectives. 'Acknowledged masterpieces...serve to set the standards, to raise the questions, to delineate the possibilities' within a realm of meaning (O'Hear, p. 58). Although they acknowledge that the canon and the tradition are still developing, they both fail, however, to do full justice to the degree to which students should, in the educational process, be introduced to a living tradition, including some of its (currently) unresolved problems and disputed questions.

One might claim that rhetoric and judgement, like teaching and learning, are correlative terms, in that they imply an intrinsic connection between communication and receptivity. We can distinguish logically, if not chronologically, two phases in the teaching act. First, as a teacher, my communication requires not only clarity about something distinctive and particular on my part, but also a receptivity from others, an openness on the part of my students. This is one aspect of their correlation. But second, if my communication is to be effective, I must be receptive to their situation and perceptions and I must attend to their communication with me.

2.4. Rhetoric Reclaimed

Aristotle used the word rhetoric in a positive sense. He had a rich and fertile understanding of the term. His analysis of rhetoric demonstrates some important connections between the art of persuasion, moral wisdom and logical reasoning. It is a fruitful source for a better understanding of the relationship between effective teaching and critical thinking. Of particular value is the way Aristotle brings out the important part played by character in the exchange of communication in the classroom. I shall treat his remarks on rhetoric both sketchily and unduly schematically because of brevity of space and in order to relate them to the issues discussed in this chapter. (I use translations by Freese, 1926 and Lawson-Tancred, 1991.)

Aristotle refers to three types of rhetoric: deliberative, forensic and epideictic. The first is concerned with what is advisable; the second with what is just; the third with what is admirable. It is the deliberative rhetoric that is most called upon within school, although there is also a need to exercise each of the other types. Aristotle also discusses three interconnected foundations for persuasion: character, emotion and reason. All three of these foundations require attention from teachers; none can be dispensed with, for they are inseparable within the act of persuasion.

According to Aristotle, audiences wish to see three qualities in an orator: good sense, virtue and goodwill. Each quality reinforces the other during the process of persuasion. If we apply each of these three qualities to the school context, the first elicits the judgement that the teacher has not been deceived by events or by reports of these events. S/he has 'read' the situation perceptively and s/he has cogent reasons for what s/he is advocating, even if all the evidence is not immediately to hand. The second quality encourages listeners to trust the teacher, because his/her motives are judged to be not self-regarding, but instead directed towards the good of the students and in harmony with sound ethical principles. Not all of these principles are necessarily spelt out at the time, but they can be assumed to be operative within his/her character. The third quality, goodwill, may be taken here to mean that, even for the sake of the good, the teacher will not seek to dominate, threaten, undermine or manipulate students in any way. Instead s/he adopts an attitude of positive regard for them and aims at their well-being, as s/he perceives this.

Aristotle reminds us first, that the mode of persuasion must be related to the political or community context. In a democracy we should beware of flattery, appeasement, demagoguery and even reliance on mere logic. The first two of these modes of persuasion are unworthy of communication in a democracy; in addition, they are variants of manipulation and inappropriate in a school. The third of these modes of persuasion constitutes an abuse of popular emotions rather than an ethical harnessing of them towards a clearly identified good. In the case of the fourth, neither the validity of an argument nor mere cleverness in a speaker renders an argument automatically persuasive; for 'logic is not audience-specific [but] persuasion is' (Garver, 1994, p. 150).

Secondly, Aristotle constantly alerts us to the important role played by argument in the art of persuasion. There must be no premature closure of the arguments, simply to convey the impression of consensus. On the other hand, it also has to be recognised that frequently, in school life in general and in the classroom in particular, decisions have to be arrived at and action taken without the benefit of prolonged enquiry, examination, reflection or debate. Schools are not research institutes, piling up evidence; they have to be satisfied with the reaching of agreement and, if fortunate, conviction, but they will rarely be in a position to claim proof for the theories or viewpoints that are the basis of decisions.

Thirdly, if trust and credibility – which does not imply gullibility on the part of audiences – are at the heart of persuasiveness, then teachers must accept that 'being a good speaker seems in many ways to depend on being a certain kind of person, rather than possessing a body of knowledge' (Garver, 1994, p. 20). If too much distance has been kept from students, or if they do not feel that they know their teacher sufficiently, then one of the springs of persuasiveness cannot function. For if showing oneself as trustworthy is an integral part of persuasiveness, then it is imperative that teachers share part of themselves, their emotions and evaluations. Such openness or vulnerability facilitates the ability of students to 'read' their teacher and must be demonstrated prior to their granting of trust.

Fourthly, Aristotle reminds orators (here we are referring to teachers) that they must be realistic in their assessment of how things appear to the various groups and classes with whom they have to work. They deal with arguments 'as they are received, rather than as they are conceived' (Garver, 1994, p. 280, quoting R. Barthes). This does not necessarily imply that each person's 'vote' counts equally in the weighing, but it does suggest that wide and regular consultation of all 'stakeholders' will help in keeping a finger on the various 'pulses' and perceptions.

This is closely related, fifthly, to Aristotle's emphasis on proper attention being given to the emotions in any attempt to be persuasive. He does not see our emotions as disconnected from our beliefs or our evaluations. Emotions are not separate from our assessment of an actual or desirable situation; emotions have a cognitive dimension. Nor is recourse to the emotions for Aristotle in contradiction to a concern for ethics. Indeed, rhetorical argument, for him, is essentially ethical, for without the ethical dimension and a concern for character, 'argument will be pure calculation, and an act of argument nothing but technique' (Garver, 1994, pp. 77, 184). Furthermore, 'the emotions are continually at work in good decisions', either being 'generated, destroyed, deflected, intensified or minimised' (Garver, 1994, pp. 108, 119).

2.5. Judgement
The act of judgement is a vital component in building up the edifice of knowledge, and opening the door to the world of

responsible behaviour. An emphasis on the importance of judgement is especially obvious in the cognitional theory of Bernard Lonergan. Judgement settles the status of an object under study for Lonergan. This can either be in the form of an affirmation or of a denial of the being of the object before the mind. Our intelligence allows us to identify and to explore possible answers to the questions prompted by our experience. Judgement is called for when we have to decide which of these possibilities is correct. Questions of truth arise at the level of judgement, which is the pivotal point in the cumulative process of coming to know, preceded by experience and understanding and followed by responsible action (Lonergan, 1958).

Quite often there is a close relationship between the judgements that we make on the work or ideas of others, and the judgements that constitute, as it were, our own being. Thus, by the way that we positively accept or reject what others say or do, we take a stand on what we judge to be really the case or really valuable in a practice. Of course, this has to be done only after we have carefully considered the relevant facts and circumstances that have a bearing on the judging of the matter. This stance might be taken as a result of careful discussion work. A judgement might be arrived at after reading appropriate literature that presents a moral dilemma during the course of a story. If students are to take up a coherent stance, they have to see the implications of the judgements they make for the situations they themselves are in now or are likely to be in soon. Thus, for example, students might ask themselves if the leading character in the story *I Am David* (Holm, 1969) is right in thinking that automatic retaliation against an aggressor is likely to lead to the lowering of oneself to the same level of behaviour as that of an aggressor. Is he correct in believing that self-respect and dignity are more important than revenge? By considering these questions they can be led to see the possible implications of such judgements for their own lives. Negative judgements here are as important as positive ones.

The judgements we make are crucial, firstly, for the self that they help us to build, secondly, for our appreciation of reality, and thirdly for our negotiation of the world we encounter. These three areas of importance are very closely related, as each affects the others; the making of judgements in one area automatically has repercussions in the other two. Unless the judgements we make are in truth our judgements, then the 'self' constituted by these judgements will not be authentic, and the world so apprehended will be ill-adapted to our inner selves, causing our responses to be inconsistent, incoherent, or difficult to maintain. Perhaps it would be better to say that there is no way through to responsible decisions and actions, except via the path of some certainty about reality. It is the role of judgement to help us decide matters of truth, certainty, reality, so that firm decisions about important matters can be taken.

The act of judging cannot just be passed on to someone else, for such a judgement does not have any purchase on the learner; it does not in any way build up the learner. S/he could not really look out at the world in the light of this passed-on judgement. How could s/he, if the judgement so accepted has not been assimilated internally and if it operates at a superficial level of her/his personality? It would be like looking out of someone else's spectacles. Personal subscription to objective standards requires a genuine personal engagement in the process leading up to judgement. You cannot coerce people to accept judgements that are not theirs, and then imagine that they are, after that, responsible for actions done in the light of these judgements. The miseducative results of what Freire calls the 'banking' concept of teaching stem from by-passing the judgements of the learner. In Freire's account, teachers deposit knowledge into tamely accepting learners whose insights are under-valued and, as a result, who become alienated from what they are taught by their superiors. In contrast, 'liberating education consists in acts of cognition, not transferrals of information' (Freire, 1972, 53).

The need for students to make their own judgements does not imply that no trust should exist between teacher and student. I have already argued above that without trust, students will not risk engagement in the subject studied, and that eliciting trust is an essential component of rhetorical activity on the part of the teacher. Although authority can be a source of prejudice if it takes the place of one's own judgement, as Gadamer pointed out (1989, p. 247), it can also be a source of truth. There are occasions when, not having sufficient experience or sufficient knowledge that is relevant to a decision, we need to accept the judgement of somebody who is better placed. This acceptance itself should, however, be a conscious judgement, which is based on past trustworthiness, at least for older students.

There are difficulties in such an advocacy of judgements. First, it might appear that training for judgements flies in the face of the fact that we need to belong to a tradition before learning to be critical of it. Freedom only arises after we have some sense of identity that is the fruit of acceptance within a community. Our individuality only emerges from our sense of belonging, of being part of a group. Encouraging critical judgements about the received tradition might seem to permit the erosion of such a support for the individual. However, it is not the dissolution of tradition that we intend as a result of judgement, but a rational, critical, responsible appropriation and modification of it, by rational contenders. There is an inevitable tension here between an initial solidarity with tradition and an ultimate openness in regard to it.

Second, there is the problem of ascertaining when is the

appropriate time and proper developmental stage for teaching students how to make judgements (and, indeed, the problem of how to do this teaching). Phasing the process carefully will be necessary, in acknowledgement of the diverse and changing capacities of students in this respect at different chronological ages and stages of maturity.

Third, there is the moral problem of ascertaining what limitations one will work under when training students to make judgements, how far they will be 'pushed' to make the 'right' judgements. If we are to educate and not to indoctrinate, then we must attend to rationality and wittingness (or knowing what is going on) on the part of learners. Only a free person can reach the truth; yet only the truth can make us free. Judgement is the link that brings the free person and the truth into close relationship. The right balance between what is accepted or believed by students, and what they must find out for themselves, is often elusive. The teacher will find it difficult to pin it down in advance of particular cases. Attempts to describe in general terms how it should and can be achieved meet resistance in the face of the recalcitrant and complex realities of classroom interaction. 'There exists a human collaboration in the pursuit and the dissemination of truth. Without some immanently generated knowledge, there would be no contributions to the collaboration. Without some beliefs, there would be no one that profited by the collaboration' (Lonergan, 1958, p. 716).

3. CONNECTIONS WITH CATHOLIC EDUCATION

I have examined two different polarities at work in schools. The first is between objective and subjective approaches to learning; the second is between rhetoric and judgement as key elements in the educational 'exchange' that takes place in the classroom. In their different ways both of these polarities illuminate important aspects of the relationship that should exist between teachers and students, for example, mutual attentiveness and respect. An understanding of both polarities also allows us an insight into crucial features that should be present in an educational 'transaction', for example, ethical communication on the part of the teacher and the intention of securing personal ownership of knowledge on the part of the student. These polarities also cast light on different aspects of Catholic education.

In Religious Education in Catholic schools, the emphasis earlier this century was on an objective approach. The Church was entrusted with the fullness of saving truth. It was expected that in Catholic schools this truth would be passed on faithfully, accurately and comprehensively. Deviation from orthodoxy was like undermining the national currency. Just as the State had the task of safeguarding the economy, so the established authorities in the Church were expected to prevent corrosive questioning, alternative interpretations, disagreement and potential heresy, all of which constituted a spiritual betrayal and therefore endangered souls. 'Error has no rights' was a slogan still in operation.

Increasingly since the Second Vatican Council the institutional Church has found it hard to 'hold the line' on a whole number of issues, to such an extent that she acknowledges a significant decline in religious practice and in levels of conformity with moral teaching. Religious Education (RE) from the late 1960s onwards frequently reflected much of the secular educational practice. It took a subjective turn, appearing to privilege experience over truth. This was just what had been feared and condemned in the modernist crisis in the early years of the twentieth century. RE became more student-centred, in giving a high priority to demonstrating the relevance of tradition to contemporary culture and in establishing links between the experience, emotions, needs and interests of students, on the one hand, and, on the other, Church teaching. I hope that my analysis in this chapter has shown the need for attention to be given to both the objective and subjective approaches to education in general and to RE in particular.

My focus on the polarity between rhetoric and judgement also brings out some necessary features of Catholic education. A retrieval of rhetoric puts an emphasis on the teacher as an exemplar of what s/he teaches and as a person who thereby elicits trust. There is a correlation between the 'message' and the medium of communication. The teacher in rhetorical mode is not to be considered merely as a source of knowledge; s/he is meant to be a witness for and an embodiment of some truth. Rhetoric also puts an emphasis on classroom dynamics as a form of exchange, where an attempt at communication intends to evoke a response from students, which in turn has an effect on the teacher. It brings out that mutuality and reciprocity should be at the heart of any hospitable space for learning if real growth is to occur.

This is where student judgement comes in; it qualifies, acts as a constraint on and offers a response to the rhetorical work of the teacher. Judgement has a role in building up the kind of person a student is becoming; it affects his or her identity. In doing so, it also facilitates a sense of ownership of the Christian message. Christian communities, far from dominating society in any universal or consistent way, appear more dispersed; their presence in the world has more of a diaspora nature. With declining numbers of Christians, Church bodies enjoy an ever-weakening influence in an increasingly secularised world. A lively sense of personal commitment to and ownership of the Christian message becomes even more vital than it was when society offered a substantial amount of religious 'capital' that could be drawn upon from a variety of social and cultural sources. Although judgements depend on students' use of some 'canonical' criteria, and although they are based on students' belonging to and provisional acceptance of some tradition, text or conceptual 'tools', they also make it possible for students to contribute to the subject of study. If divine revelation is not appreciated until it receives a response from humanity, so a tradition is not living unless it is open to the present insights and judgements of those who engage with it. To emphasise the important part played by judgement in our individual and collective growth – in faith matters as in others – is at the same time to ensure that education fosters contributions from students, not mere repetition. The kind of ownership made possible through acts of judgement allows assimilation to lead to transformation, both of the students and of what is studied.

RECOMMENDED READING

Freese, J. H., translation of Aristotle's *Art of Rhetoric* (London: Loeb Classical Library, Heinemann, 1926).

Freire, P., *Pedagogy of the Oppressed* (London: Penguin, 1972).

Gadamer, H-G., *Truth and Method* (trans.) Joel Weinsheimer & Donald Marshall, second revised edition (New York: Crossroad 1989).

Garver, E., Aristotle's *Rhetoric: An Art of Character* (Chicago: University of Chicago Press, 1994).

Holm, A., *I am David* (London: Puffin, 1969).

Lawson-Tancred, H., translation of Aristotle's *Art of Rhetoric* (London: Penguin, 1991).

Lonergan, B., *Insight* (London: Longmans, Green & Co., 1958).

O'Hear, A., 'Values, education and culture', in *Education, Values and Culture*, The Victor Cook Memorial Lectures (ed.) John Haldane (Centre for Philosophy and Public Affairs: University of St Andrews, 1992).

Quinton, A., 'Culture, Education and Values' in *Education, Values and Culture*, The Victor Cook Memorial Lectures (ed.) John Haldane (Centre for Philosophy and Public Affairs: University of St Andrews, 1992).

CONCLUSION

The various metaphors for school that have been examined here all vie for dominance in the thinking and practical decision-making of those responsible for Catholic education. There are four aspects to this contention. First, there are tensions between the school and the communities that provide the source of each particular metaphor. Families, for example, may feel that the school does not appreciate their own perspective on various matters, such as discipline, the curriculum, homework or uniform. They may complain that their views and rights are not respected, that consultation is inadequate, and that their voice is insufficiently heeded. Conversely, teachers may feel that they receive too little support from parents, that their efforts in school are undermined by what gets said and done at home, or that parents fail to exercise their responsibilities, for example with regard to spiritual and moral development. Although not inevitable, such tensions between families and school are common.

With regard to relations between school and the business world, employers may feel that teachers are insufficiently aware of economic realities, do not prepare students to be reliable workers, fail to build up the entrepreneurial spirit, and even fall short on basic education. In parallel fashion, teachers may complain that undue pressure is imposed on schools to give priority to economic concerns over alternative ones, for example, the aesthetic and cultural, the philosophical and the spiritual. They may feel that employers take too narrow a view of education, that they expect too passive a workforce and that they do not take kindly to schools offering a critique of the current workings and the prevailing values of capitalism. When business management methods are applied to schools, teachers sometimes feel that inappropriate and even alien ideologies are imported at the same time, with effects that are injurious to the practice of education. There are occasions when too much attention given to efficiency can deflect attention from ethics. Although not inevitable, these tensions are frequently displayed in relations between school and the world of business.

Without going into detail here, it will also be apparent that there are similar tensions, with contrasting and sometimes contradictory perspectives and expectations of each other, that arise both between schools and the Church and between schools and the political community to which they belong. These tensions have always been present and they are not about to disappear in the foreseeable future.

Second, there are tensions arising within a school as to the degree to which each of the metaphors should be given scope for application; questions here might relate either to their *legitimacy* in the school context, or to their *practicality*, given the particular circumstances and the force of obstructing factors. As for the question of legitimacy, some teachers might feel that, to seek to make a school reflect features of the family is an inappropriate goal, distorting their work into something quite different from their perception of what it ought to be. Conversely, they might believe such an attempt would constitute an unwarranted and unduly paternalistic course if adopted by the school, one that exceeds the limits of its jurisdiction and interferes with the rights of parents. As for the question of practicality, it could be argued that, however desirable it may be to make schools places with a strong family feeling and atmosphere, down-to-earth realities prevent this being achieved to any marked degree. Many factors inhibit a family atmosphere in the school context. The following might be cited as examples:

- large numbers of people in confined and sometimes uncomfortable accommodation;
- intrusive timetables that do not match the rhythms of normal life;
- the compulsory and formal nature of schooling;
- the fleeting nature of acquaintance between some students, especially older ones, and their teachers.

All these are compounded by:

- the sheer diversity of experience and viewpoint that is evident in the composition of many school communities.

Similar issues arise about both legitimacy and practicality when there are attempts to interpret school in the light of a business, a Church or a political community.

Third, there is contention between those who advocate the relative priority of one particular metaphor for school over the others. Thus, different members of staff or of the Board of Governors/Managers, despite accepting that a school necessarily has to be a 'mixed' institution, that is, one with multiple dimensions, simultaneously reflecting at least some aspects of a family, a business, a Church and a political community, nevertheless expect their preferred metaphor to predominate over all the others, believing that this best expresses and facilitates the true nature of school.

Fourth, it should not be assumed that there is unanimity or consensus about how the originating communities that lie behind the metaphors should be interpreted or understood. Normative discussion about the family, business and the Church is now often as inescapably contentious as has always been the case over the ideals that should govern the political community. Arguments are conducted over the respective nature and purpose, as well as over the rights and duties, of each of these human groupings. These arguments already exist with regard to each type of community, separate from and without reference to schooling; but they are compounded when brought into contact with one another in an educational context. The practice of education itself has always been one of the most debated of terms, both with regards to its constituent features, its guiding norms and its actual achievements.

Adams suggested that society can best be understood as an extended argument, since living traditions pre-suppose rival interpretations. Good societies enable the argument to continue so that the possibilities and limits of the tradition can be exposed. The great danger, however, is that the success of a tradition will stop its growth and in reaction some may deny the necessity of tradition for their lives. The truthfulness of a tradition is tested in its ability to form people who are ready to put the tradition into question, or at least to recognize when it is being put into question by a rival tradition. (Stanley Hauerwas [commenting on Richard Adams' novel *Watership Down*] in *The Community of Character* [University of Notre Dame Press, 1981], p. 14.)

How is a Catholic school leader to respond in the light of – and feeling the heat of – the contentious nature of schooling in general and of Catholic schooling in particular? One response might be to acknowledge that s/he has a major role in facilitating the extended argument that Hauerwas sees as integral to the continuation of any living tradition. Principals benefit from both the support *and* the challenge offered by the different and often conflicting perspectives of the family, business, the Church, the political community and the academy. Without the opportunities and pressures brought about by these ever-shifting sources of support and challenge, a school will be a poorer educational environment and it will represent less effectively the many different dimensions of life. The competing claims of family, business, Church and the political community ensure that the education provided in the academy is broad, multi-faceted and touched by an awareness of alternative ways of thinking and acting. In this way, what is experienced in school will prepare students all the more effectively for life in a pluralist democracy and it should equip them to participate more fully in a pluralist Church.

It has been an implicit theme of this book that the contentious nature of Catholic schools is not merely an *accidental* feature, but rather one that is *essential* to their healthy functioning, painful and wearisome though this contention will be for the people who are responsible for steering their way through it. Among the many qualities and skills required of Catholic school leaders must be included a willingness to entertain criticism and an adeptness in responding to it. Disagreement and debate prevent any temptation towards institutional idolatry and they render complacency impossible. Given that Catholic schools are the focus of such contention, it should be a cause of continuing wonder, admiration and praise that so many of their leaders manage to respond with their ideals intact, with humility and humanity in the face of shortcomings, and with the kind of hope in the future that invites and empowers others to engage with the mission.

Appendix

A. Write a dialogue between (a) someone who is well-informed about and firmly committed to Catholic schools, and (b) someone who does not approve of the existence of such separate schools. Draw on the strongest ideas and arguments for each side, including your own responses and perspective where appropriate. The point of the dialogue is not to have a clear victory for one side or the other; rather, the point is to engage the issues in an active and critical manner.

B. From your reading and from your own experience, which aspect of the theory of Catholic education is most influential? (or most reflected in practice?) and which principle appears most contentious, encountering opposition, or suffering either misunderstanding or lack of commitment in Catholic schools?

C. Which part of Catholic teaching is most helpful to you in your work as an educator and which part is most problematical? Explain why/how in each case.

D. Identify an unresolved problem or question of significance for the task of Catholic education and show how an understanding of the relevant key concepts can clarify the work involved in addressing one of the priorities of Catholic school leaders.

E. Which official (Roman or national) guidance on Catholic education has greatest significance for Catholic school leaders at the beginning of the twenty-first century?